Working for Wages

Working for Wages

On the Road in the Fifties

Peter Browning

Great West Books Lafayette, California

Cover design by Larry Van Dyke

Manufactured in the Unites States of America

Library of Congress Cataloging-in-Publication Data

Browning, Peter, 1928–
Working for wages : on the road in the fifties / Peter Browning
p. cm.
ISBN 0-944220-15-0 (Paperback : alk. paper)
1. Browning, Peter, 1928– 2. Truck drivers—United States—Biography.
3. Working class—United States—Biography.
4. United States—Description and travel. I. Title.
HD8039.M7952U527 2003
388.3'21—dc21
2003000810

Front cover illustration:
Author with a Brockway and two Divcos, on U.S. 350 between La Junta and Trinidad, Colorado, Christmas Day 1953.

Great West Books
P.O. Box 1028
Lafayette, CA 94549-1028
Phone & Fax: (925) 283-3184
E-mail: peter@greatwestbooks.com
Web site: www.greatwestbooks.com

Contents

Introduction

I was born in Cleveland, Ohio on the last day of 1928. Both my parents were college graduates, my upbringing—and values and standards—were upper-middle class, and in the normal course of events I would have acquired a "higher education" and quite likely proceeded into one of the professions.

I made a couple of stabs at college, but dropped out both times after a few weeks. I had several dull jobs, and then—in the young man's tradition of perversity—I did what was most inimical to my own interests: I joined the Navy.

The Navy was dead time—a period of going through the motions while waiting to get out. Once I was free again I reentered college, sat through one class, and dropped out while I was still ahead. I hadn't the least idea of what I might do in life—or with my life—and the urge to travel was my primary motivation.

After an eight-week stint as a deckhand on an iron-ore carrier on the Great Lakes, I signed on with the "Old Man" to make a one-way trip from Detroit to Los Angeles, with no notion of what I would do when I got to the Coast—and I wound up driving for the Old Man for nine and a half years. My companions on the job were not the sort of people I had known before. They thought and acted differently, and had different expectations and prospects in life. What we had in common were travel fever, no plans for the future, and no homes. The real home was the job—constant motion and a succession of hotel rooms. The future was the next trip. The knowledge that there would be several trips in a row constituted our version of stability and permanence.

I was on the road for the Old Man from May 1949 to December 1958, and during that period drove new cars and trucks from Detroit to Los Angeles 130 times. When I started, the country was still recovering from the Great Depression and the Second World War. Nine and a half years later, millions of people had realized their onward-and-upward aspirations: a new car, a house in the suburbs, a good job, money in the bank—and the kids had braces on their teeth.

The world passed us by. The end of the fifties saw us no better off than at the beginning. There was motion without progress, and nothing to show for our labors. We were older and tireder, wiser and more cynical. I acquired some of the outlook of my companions while retaining my own, and gained an education of the sort that cannot be taught but must be learned.

What follows is an anecdotal account of who we were, how we lived, and how we talked. None of these tales is precisely true in every respect, yet none is false. Most of the names have been changed to protect the innocent and the guilty alike.

When the Old Man folded up his tent we were left stranded, but we were not without resources. Our instincts, our experience, our habits, the very history of the country showed us the way. We went west once more, to start life anew.

Pilgrim's Progress

All in the golden afternoon
  Full leisurely we glide,
For both our oars with little skill
  By little arms are plied
While little hands make vain pretense
  Our wanderings to guide.

Alice's Adventures in Wonderland
Lewis Carroll

Life is just one damned thing after another.

I was discharged from the Navy in January 1949, two weeks past my twentieth birthday. I reentered college, sat through one class, and dropped out while I was still ahead. In late March I signed on as deckhand on the *S.S. Youngstown* of the Interlake Steamship Company. From Allouez or Two Harbors at the western end of Lake Superior, the *Youngstown* hauled iron ore to a Lake Michigan or Lake Erie port, and returned empty, in a week.

In late May we were downbound in the Detroit River with a load of ore destined for Cleveland. The mail boat came out from Detroit and rode alongside us for a few minutes, while we lowered a bucket over the side to pick up mail and newspapers. I read the entire paper, and was intrigued by an ad in the 'Transportation' column that read "Cars delivered, drivers wanted." Working on the Lakes had already become dull routine, and driving around the country sounded like the life for me. In a moment I made up my mind, and I informed the First Mate that my career as a steamboater was at an end. I signed off in Cleveland, and grabbed the bus to Detroit.

Although Detroit was but a five-hour ride from Cleveland, it might just as well have been on a foreign strand. My state of mind was such that any departure, for anywhere, was sufficient to arouse an intense interest in whatever the world might provide. All that was needed was to start out, and at once I was fulfilled, satisfied beyond question that I was embarked on a worthy undertaking. The value of the journey lay in the motion itself.

I spent the night in a shabby walk-up hotel near the Detroit bus station, and in the morning rode a municipal bus out Grand River Avenue to the establishment whose ad had caught my eye. There were several such businesses operating in Detroit, but their ads were more prosaic, mentioning cities or states to which one might drive a car as one's own (Cars to all points, Cal., Fla., N.Y., Ariz.), and perhaps some of the conditions governing the arrangement (Deposit req., gas allow.). But none had the appeal of the legend, simultaneously clear and cryptic: Cars delivered, drivers wanted. This turned out to be the Dealers Driveaway Service, consisting of two rooms above a hardware store.

The outer room contained a battered table, several wobbly wooden chairs, and a torn calendar on a wall from which the institutional-green paint was peeling to expose gray wallboard. On the table were the tops of coffee tins, their edges bent upward to form ashtrays, all of them overflowing with crushed butts. Several men in their twenties or thirties slumped in the chairs, idly smoking or flipping through the pages of ancient magazines. The room was so dreary and its occupants seemed so exhausted that I hesitated to enter, feeling that my expectations were utterly ruined. Obviously this was not the port from which I might sail off across the country.

The door to the inner room, the office, was wide open. Seated at a desk was a woman of about forty-five, with dyed reddish hair. I stood in the outer room, uncertain as to what I should do, and looked about for some clue to the correct procedure. When the woman spotted me, she shouted, "All right, what the hell do *you* want?" Before I could reply she beckoned me into the office, ordered me to sit down, and asked me where I wanted to go and how old was I. I answered that I had seen the ad in the paper, couldn't say where I wanted to go until I knew where there was to go, and that I was twenty-one—which was lying by only one year. Immediately she asked when I was born, and I told her without hesitation, pushing it back one year.

"Either you're telling the truth or you think awful fast," she said. Either way, I took it as a compliment.

Her name was Kay Daley, she had been in this business since sometime in the thirties, and she ran her little enclave like a benevolent dictatorship—using, instead of an iron hand, a loud voice and a penchant for strong language. She was sipping bourbon from a paper cup, and hinted that she had a cannon in the desk drawer. She seemed pleased that I was taken aback by her blunt approach. Once it became apparent that I was not a yahoo, some bum off the streets who would give her a hard time, she moderated her tone and explained the realities underlying her ad—an ad that ran constantly, regardless of the volume of her business. In short, there were no jobs to be had. She functioned as the liaison between the owners of cars who wished to have them driven to distant points, and people desirous of getting to those points with minimal expense. Depending on the destination and the time of year, the driver had to pay for part or all of the gas. This deal was supposed to be beneficial to all, except that someone who was broke, and therefore most in need of cheap transportation, was precisely the person who would not be able to get it. You had to put up a modest deposit, and you had to buy gas to reach your destination. The needy got nothing, and nothing was free.

I was downcast but not disheartened. I had plenty of money, and though there was no job I was set on going somewhere. My only need was to choose a destination—Miami, Dallas, Phoenix, Seattle, even Anchorage if I felt adventurous.

Kay Daley solved the problem for me. Interspersed with answering the phone, cursing the loungers in the outer room, and uttering caustic asides on the stupidity and venality of mankind and the sad state of society in general, she casually informed me that there was a job of sorts, going on a "caravan" to Los Angeles. There would be modest pay—she didn't have the figures at hand—perhaps some of the expenses would be covered—she was fuzzy about the details—and furthermore, it was only superficially a job.

The word "caravan" conjured up pictures of camels, and questioning didn't help much. I learned that it was to be a caravan of "milk wagons" —which might as well have been camels. The mystery became more profound when Kay said that I would need a chauffeur's license because the job was run under I.C.C. regulations.

I acquired a chauffeur's license without difficulty, and by mid-afternoon I was back at Kay's, smoking in the outer room while exchanging rumors with the other loungers. We were waiting for the caravan man to arrive. Now and again Kay would send someone out for coffee. One of those times she stuck her head out, surveyed us with contemptuous amusement, and said, *sotto voce,* "What a sorry-looking bunch of bastards this is." And then, loudly, "Take your hands out of your pockets—you'll go crazy that way!"

The caravan man was the only person whom Kay Daley regarded with respect. When he wasn't around she referred to him as the "Old Man" or "Father," but they were friendly terms. The Old Man arrived and took us prospective drivers out for a driving test in a rented car. The test was simple: if you could control the car, stay in your lane, and manage to make a few turns, the Old Man would take you on.

At first I mistook the Old Man for the personnel agent of the concern that transported these milk wagons to the Coast, not realizing that he *was* the concern—the entire business rolled into one man. He told us the details of the caravan. There would be eight drivers, each with two vehicles hooked together on a towbar. The Old Man would buy all the gas, and would pay us $75 wages. There were a couple of catches, though. From the $75 he would deduct $16 for our lodging en route—predicated on eight nights at two dollars a night. There would also be a three-dollar deduction for the Teamsters Union. One of the drivers, bolder or more knowledgeable than the rest of us, questioned the payment to the union, since it did not seem that there were any benefits to be derived from giving the union its due. "It's a trip fee," he was told, and that was that. No one wanted to press the issue, for fear of being left behind—a classic case of beggars unable to choose.

The next morning we met at the lot where the vehicles were; it was the backyard of an abandoned house near the corner of Michigan and Wyoming. There were expressions of disbelief when we had our first look at the milk wagons. They were Divcos, and in our eyes lacked only hard rubber tires and horses to be true milk wagons. I realized that I had seen many Divcos, for they were used mainly by dairies and were found in many cities. They were boxy, had sloping fronts with a faintly English look to them, high windshields, and folding doors on either side. Ours, being factory fresh, were painted with a prime coat—a dull brown. Under the hoods were the smallest vehicle engines we had ever seen: four cylinders, about the size of a Model-T engine, rated at 37.5 horsepower and looking as though they belonged in lawn mowers.

This model of Divco weighed 4,500 pounds, and it was inconceivable that such a paltry engine could haul 9,000 pounds across the country. There was a bit of grumbling, and a rumor that the whole deal was a hoax—speculation that since we obviously couldn't drive these milk wagons clear to the Coast, our true destination must be some obscure, undesirable place—perhaps a body shop in southern Indiana, or a tank town down in the hills. When we got there, the Old Man would holler "April Fool," they'd pay us off in skim milk, and there we'd be—up a dry creek with half a canoe and no paddle. What made us doubly suspicious was that there were Indiana transport plates on the vehicles. Obviously somebody was up to no good.

But what the hell, if we didn't take on this job what would we do? No one backed down, and by noon we had the outfit on the road. The Old Man led the way. Halfway back in the caravan was a middle-aged man named Henry Gerber, who was nervous and excited and threw his weight around a lot, so I figured he was the boss. Running on the tail end was Jerry Apperson, who along with Henry had been on the job before the war. The other five of us had come out of Kay Daley's, and were making the trip one way. I was the youngest; there was a talkative, brash, but likable guy just out of college who said that he had some sort of a government job lined up in Burma; a skinny wiseacre in his mid-twenties with a pimply face and a sneering way of talking; a guy wearing a black leather jacket and a motorcycle-rider's cap; and a scrawny, beat-down silent hillbilly of about forty. The last three said that they were going to L.A. to look for work, because times were hard in Detroit and it was supposed to be more comfortable starving to death in California than in Michigan—and besides, the girls were prettier and more friendly out there. The hillbilly was so poorly off that his gear consisted of just one change of clothes, wrapped in newspaper and tied with string.

We headed out the Willow Run Expressway on a warm, windy spring day. It was a good thing that we had a divided four-lane road to practice on, because two Divcos on a towbar is the worst-handling outfit ever invented. Every irregularity in the road made me think that I was going to lose control, and that my Divcos would take a mind to lurch into the nearest ditch or charge off into a muddy field and tear down fences. When I went over a bump, the front truck leaped to the left and the rear one sashayed right. Then I'd over-correct, and both trucks headed in opposite directions. After I did that several times running, my outfit was going down the road like a sidewinder, seeming to be simultaneously in both lanes and onto the right shoulder.

I looked down at the speedometer and saw that I was doing only thirty. Top speed in that model was forty-five, but we traveled more than five hundred miles before anyone had nerve enough to drive them that fast. I prided myself on being a good driver, but the Divcos made me feel like an inept beginner who lacked the ability to drive around the block much less across the continent. But the Old Man plainly was having a tougher struggle than I, and in the rearview mirrors I could see dust fly as the hookups behind me hit the shoulder.

In 1949 the expressway ran about thirty miles, from the Detroit city limits to just west of Ypsilanti. It had been built during the war to service the Ford bomber plant at Willow Run. At the end of the expressway we turned onto U.S. 112, which was then the main road from Detroit to Chicago, and wound away through the green countryside, through Saline and Clinton and the Irish Hills, where we stopped and climbed the tower to get the view, then down the hill at Moscow and on to Jonesville where we stopped at a delicatessen and bought a lunch of sandwiches, doughnuts, and coffee.

Henry said that this was the first time, bar none, that anybody had ever tried taking hookups of Divcos over the road, and somebody said they shoulda left those puddlejumping bastards be. A man working for a dairy drove by in a Divco and hollered out that he didn't know his truck had so many kids, and one of the drivers gave him the finger and yelled back that they were misbegotten and ugly as sin but they were all we had and if he didn't like it he could go piss up a rope.

Between Bronson and Sturgis one of the Divcos had a blowout. None of the trucks had spare tires, just spare rims. Henry and Jerry took one of the hookups apart, and they and the Old Man took a single Divco back the way we'd come to buy a new tire. We were parked by a roadside café, so we spent three hours drinking too much coffee and trying to make out with the waitress and feeding the jukebox. That was when jukeboxes still had only ten records, and those hadn't been changed since the Flood. The best side was "Sugar Blues" by Clyde McCoy, which got a pretty fair workout. The waitress sure got tired of all our dumb bullshit, but she kidded along anyway because she was way out in the sticks and there wasn't much excitement.

By the time the Old Man returned with a new tire we were ready for a bit of excitement ourselves, so we whipped up our Divcos and got the show on the road again. At Mottville we turned south and went into Indiana—and were enlightened by the roadside prophecy.

Spring
has sprung
the grass
has riz
where
last year's
careless
drivers iz
Burma Shave

We plugged along until well after dark to reach the town of Rochester, where we put up for the night in the Karn Hotel. We were considerably surprised when we found that we had to double-up in the beds. It didn't seem as though we were getting full value for the two dollars a night that was coming out of the seventy-five that wasn't enough to begin with. We did some muttering amongst ourselves, but we didn't have any leverage so there wasn't any use complaining to the Old Man. Somebody said that what the job needed was a strong union and that the union was the workingman's best friend, and somebody else said amen to that—but we didn't belong to the right church.

The next morning we went along in good style until we were thirty-five miles west of Rochester. At a stop sign the skinny wiseacre smacked into the rear of another hookup, smashing fenders and grills and breaking headlights. We took the two damaged trucks and one undamaged one back to Rochester, stayed there overnight, left the two damaged trucks to be repaired, and tried it again the next morning. The Old Man gave the wiseacre bus fare back to Detroit. That guy must have been our Jonah, because after that we had no more trouble.

It took a long time. When we crossed the Mississippi our doubts were dispelled: we believed that it wasn't a bad joke, and that we were going to the Coast after all. We stayed in small towns, in old two-story country hotels that charged about a dollar and a half a head. There was Rushville, Illinois, where we made an early stop even though we could have gone on to Quincy (Henry gave us a knowing wink and said those river towns were something else and the Old Man didn't want us to stay overnight in Quincy for fear we'd get all fucked up); Atchison, Kansas, on the Missouri River, and that was the beginning of the West; Stafford, Kansas, on a hot night in an old brick hotel above the bank; La Junta, Colorado, where the water was so hard you couldn't drink it and couldn't work up a lather with it; Las Vegas, New Mexico, in the Castaneda Hotel down by the depot, with the switch engine banging cars all night in the yards; Gallup, New Mexico, where we were surprised to see how the Indians looked and dressed—nothing like in the movies; Prescott, Arizona, where in the evening we sat on the benches in the courthouse park and watched the girls and the traffic go by; and the Sunset Motel right at the edge of Banning, California, just after we came up out of the desert; and on the last day it was an easy 85-mile jaunt into L.A.

The sun was shining and it was sure good to see the orange trees and the palm trees and to get shed of those Divcos. The Old Man paid us off, and somebody figured out that the trip was about 2,500 miles, had taken eleven days, that after deductions of three dollars for the union and sixteen dollars for hotels we got gross pay of fifty-six dollars, which was about five dollars a day or two and a quarter cents a mile—and that's a starvation wage no matter how you cut it. A man would be better off not knowing any mathematics.

I had no clear idea of what I would do next, or of where I might go next. For the lack of any impetus I suppose that I might have wandered back home to Ohio. But life cannot possibly stagnate as long as you do not resist the flow of events. Two days after we arrived, Henry phoned me to say that there were three hookups back in Detroit, and did I want to make another trip—for one hundred dollars this time, but with the same deductions. I was all for it. The Old Man put Henry, me, and Floyd Isaacs—the guy with the black leather jacket and motorcycle rider's cap—on the train, and we rode back to Detroit in style.

In Detroit, Henry hired a driver through Kay Daley. He was Vic Szafranski, headed for the Coast to escape a bad marriage and an even worse divorce. When the judge in Port Huron told him that he would have to cough up $125 a month alimony, he quit his hacking job and went down to Detroit to get a driveout car to anywhere—and fell into the Old Man's operation. We went on down to Rochester to pick up the damaged Divcos, but they weren't quite ready and we had to stay there two nights. If we'd had to live in a small town like Rochester we would have gone west for good—way up in the big sky, pushing the clouds around. As the words of the old song have it, Saint Peter woulda been the strawboss then.

There simply wasn't anything to do in Rochester. At Henry's suggestion we went to Lake Manitou, a mile outside of town, but the vacation season wasn't yet under way, and few people were there.

There was one knockout of a girl in a white bikini, sunbathing on the beach. We almost wore holes in that bikini by staring at it. The girl was from Chicago, and said that she was an "interpretive dancer," currently performing at the only place in Rochester to offer live entertainment—a tavern that charged double for the beer.

We went there that evening, and watched the girl fling herself around to the accompaniment of a scratchy phonograph record. She didn't dance as good as she looked. Her moves were a combination of flamenco, belly-dancing, and the Jersey Bounce. We praised everything she did and bought her a lot of drinks, but no one got to first base. The damaged Divcos were ready the next morning, and we were on our way. A couple of years later that tavern burned to the ground—probably good riddance.

The trip was without incident. The Old Man said that he expected to have more business soon, so I went home to Ohio and waited for his call. "Soon" turned out to be ten weeks. It wasn't until after Labor Day that the Old Man sent word to go to Detroit. That was the beginning of something I'd never planned on: I drove for the Old Man for more than nine years.

Easy Work

> The best business you can go into you will find on your father's farm or in his workshop. If you have no family or friends to aid you, and no prospect opened to you there, turn your face to the great West, and there build up a home and fortune.
>
> ***To Aspiring Young Men***
> **Horace Greeley**

Driving for the Old Man, at the outset, was a job that had none of the drawbacks normally associated with working. As far as I was concerned, shuttling back and forth between Detroit and Los Angeles was a permanent vacation. I had no responsibilities beyond driving my own hookup. The convoy leader (sometime early in the game the word 'caravan' metamorphosed into 'convoy') handled all the details: gas bills, hotels, when to stop, where to park, when to get up in the morning. The physical effort and discomfort of driving bothered me very little, and all the rest of it was a lark.

The pay wasn't much, but my expenses weren't much either: three meals and two packs of cigarettes a day, a movie once in a while, some magazines and paperback books, occasionally another pair of khakis or a sport shirt at Penney's or Monkey Wards. I wasn't maintaining a home, so there was no rent, no utilities to pay, few of the normal expenses of settled life; just eats and smokes, and if you didn't booze it up and weren't trying to feed a lot of other faces, you could even put money in the bank.

As far as anyone could ever make out, the Old Man didn't need to be in business. He was in his early sixties, and was well off. He had been born in Kankakee, Illinois in 1885, grew up in Chicago, and moved to California with his parents in 1901. He and his father started an auto dealership and were in on the ground floor of the automobile age. The Old Man participated in some early auto trips and races, and had known Barney Oldfield.

By the middle twenties the Old Man was the regional distributor for Jordan automobiles. Kay Daley and some of the caravan leaders who had worked for the Old Man before the war said that he had been a millionaire, but there was no way to prove or disprove that. The Old Man was always close-mouthed about his financial affairs, past or present. When the stock market went smash in 1929, the Jordan Automobile Company went smash along with it—mainly because the Jordan brothers had gone south with the money.

Of course the Old Man went down with the wreckage, but soon afterward he hit on the idea of transporting cars rather than selling them as a way to make an honest buck. He started a driveaway business in the early thirties, with the help of his two brothers, and by the late thirties he had a flourishing operation. From 1938 through 1941 the Old Man took all the new Hudsons for southern California and Arizona over the road from Detroit, and he also transported Studebakers to Los Angeles from South Bend, Indiana. He ran caravans of twenty to twenty-five hookups, manned entirely by one-way drivers except for the 'pilot' and 'mechanic,' who led and brought up the rear, and drove single cars so that they could run up and down the line. In those last few years before the war the Old Man was transporting 3,500 to 4,000 cars a year, and even if he didn't get rich he must have been doing all right.

The war killed his business, but he started up again in 1946, transported a flock of DeSoto taxicabs to the Yellow Cab Company in Los Angeles, then folded up in 1947 when he couldn't get any more business. But the Old Man wasn't the sort of guy who could just sit around and count his money. He needed to be up and doing, even though the best he could manage was a one-horse business when he started going again in 1949, and the only vehicles he could get were Divcos. It was a good hobby for him—kept him from getting old and dying.

There was an inexhaustible supply of one-way drivers, in good times and bad. When I became a convoy leader, I could count on finding a cluster of anxious, worried men at Kay Daley's—usually men with no money and no prospects, waiting around on the off chance that they could get on a convoy going to the Coast.

I met Vic Szafranski on that first trip after Labor Day 1949. He lived in Port Huron, had just been divorced, had to give up his car and other property in the settlement, and was supposed to ante up $125 a month in alimony. He was double-damned if he was going to work his ass off for that no-good cunt of an ex-wife of his, so he quit his job and went down to Detroit, his only immediate desire being to put a lot of miles between himself and Port Huron. Why go to Los Angeles? Well, L.A. is farther than Miami and warmer than Seattle. But most important, there is only one direction in the United States that amounts to anything, and that's West. North is for Eskimos, South is for the birds, and East is the place everybody eventually will leave to go west.

Going west is traditional. It's the way you head when your life has broken into pieces and you want to find some place where you can put the pieces back together—but in a new pattern. It's where you go when you get restless doing the same old thing day in and day out, or when you want to have one last fling before getting into harness. And when all the demands of civilization weigh too heavily on you, and you can't cut it any more, you can always kick over the traces and pull a Huckleberry Finn—"Light out for the territory." And that means West.

Most of those who became steady drivers for the Old Man started out the same way I did, by making a one-way trip with the intention of staying in California. But when you got to L.A., you either asked to make another trip or were invited to make one, and then another trip after that—and it was one trip after another. Now and again the Old Man would try the approach of advertising in the newspaper and hiring some drivers in L.A., but the men he hired seldom worked out well. We suspected that the Old Man made the job sound better than it really was, and the reality came as such a great shock that the men he hired usually skedaddled after one or two trips. Those who started out as one-way drivers had no illusions, and also knew that any changes could only be for the better.

One of the few good drivers the Old Man hired in L.A. was Jim Baumann. Jim was also one of the few on the job who had had considerable heavy-duty driving experience. His previous job had been eighteen months of driving a semi-dump on a government construction project on Guam, where—according to Jim—he made better than a thousand dollars a month. No one knew what possessed him to come as far down as working for the chintzy wages the Old Man paid, but he stuck on the job for about a year.

The Divcos we had in the fall of 1949 were a slightly different breed from the ones of the first two trips. They were the same size and had the same engine, but they were geared differently. The top speed was thirty-five, and because they were meant for house-to-house delivery they had peculiar controls. We called them stand-up Divcos, because they could be driven either standing or sitting. The clutch and brake were in the same pedal—clutch engaged when it was out, becoming disengaged when depressed, and brakes coming on when it was depressed further. A tricky aspect of this arrangement was that the brakes would lock up if the pedal was depressed past a certain point when you were in neutral, so that if you pushed the clutch in too far while shifting gears, the Divco would make an unwanted stop.

Beginners on stand-up Divcos occasionally found themselves stranded in intersections or halfway up hills, having inadvertently locked the brakes while shifting gears. The only way to make your Divco go again was to put it in any gear and depress the clutch-brake further still, which unlocked it. Separate from the clutch-brake was a slow-down brake, a four-foot-long handle sticking up through the floorboard like misplaced plumbing. To reduce speed, you grabbed the handle and hauled back on it, after the fashion of a wagon-driver retarding the speed of his rig on a downgrade. There was a gas pedal on the floor to use while standing, another gas pedal in the customary place to use while sitting, twisting the gearshift knob forward was also a gas feed, and there was a hand throttle on the dashboard.

This strange collection of levers, pedals, and buttons led one frustrated beginner to call the Divcos "those Chinese Mixmasters." They were an outfit meant to be driven by a crazy man with two left hands and the seven-year itch. The most unnerving experience in a stand-up Divco was to have a traffic light change to red when you were right on top of it. You instinctively slammed your right foot against a bare, brakeless floorboard, and then became so flustered that you couldn't think of the proper combination. With hunched-up shoulders, and hands frozen to the wheel, you sailed through the intersection, certain that the day of retribution was at hand.

Stand-up Divcos required a ten-day trip, and we developed an invariable schedule of overnight stops—barring breakdowns or bad weather. Rochester, Indiana; Quincy, Illinois; Ottawa and Dodge City, Kansas; Raton, Las Vegas, and Gallup, New Mexico; Prescott, Arizona; and Banning, California. The schedule was dictated, in part, by I.C.C. regulations. Commercial drivers were allowed ten consecutive hours of driving time, to be followed by at least eight hours off duty before driving another ten. Another restriction limited driving time to seventy hours in eight consecutive days. By the time we reached Raton we had put in forty-seven hours in five days. We could have driven ten hours the sixth and seventh days, but—to be legal—we then could have driven only three hours the eighth day. So we had to put in a short day somewhere along the line to make the logbook come out right.

It took us about three hours to go from Raton to Las Vegas in stand-up Divcos, and then we had the rest of the day to ourselves. Even with that schedule we often stretched the logbook to make ten hours cover twelve to fifteen hours of driving. But we were certainly more nearly legal than most truckers. I.C.C. logbooks have had just one major effect: drivers become adept at filling out logbooks to make their trips look legal, no matter what they actually are doing. It was common practice to keep two logbooks. One, which outlined a plausible trip, was turned in at the home terminal; and the other was kept up to date while on the road, to be shown to I.C.C. inspectors or the cops.

The Old Man resurrected several of the pilots who had run caravans for him before the war. Henry Gerber was a natural, because he couldn't drink due to an ulcer. The next old-timer to show up was Jack Blue, a man in his middle fifties, heavyset and paunchy. He told endless stories of running caravans before the war, about the places he'd been and the people he knew, of his exploits and adventures—cautionary tales about how to make your way in the world and about the perils of being on the road. It was impossible to distinguish fact from fantasy, or to be certain that Jack *ever* told the truth. Often he would start a story, tell just enough to arouse our interest, but never take it to a conclusion or make the point that had seemed to be forthcoming. Part way through the story he would stop abruptly and give us a big wink and a sly grin, as if to say "We know what it's all about, don't we?"

When I met Jack he carried a bindle instead of a suitcase. It was simply a blanket, with his spare clothes and shaving gear rolled up inside, and the ends of the roll connected with a belt to form a horseshoe-shaped bundle that he could sling across his shoulders. He said that it was the only way to travel, much more practical than a suitcase because it wouldn't handicap you if you had to move in a hurry. Jack made it sound as if we suddenly might be made destitute by some catastrophic event, and would find ourselves hopping freight trains and living in hobo jungles.

But to demonstrate that he wasn't a bum, Jack told us all about the great jobs he'd had, and how all the people he'd worked for would be glad to have him back again. At one time, he said, he'd been the private chauffeur for Al Jolson. He got the job by answering an ad for a chauffeur and bodyguard. When he stepped through the door at the place of application, he was jumped from behind by two men wielding blackjacks. Of course he handily beat the bejesus out of them, and the demonstration of his talent constituted a first-rate reference. Jolson, who observed the action through a one-way mirror, hired Jack on the spot. And Jack told us of all the times he drove Jolson from Los Angeles to Palm Springs, with Jolson in the back seat yelling "Faster faster!" And how Jolson was a great boozer and whoremaster, and democratic to boot, so that Jack was always awash in a mixture of whiskey and girls, and came near to ruining his health trying to keep up with the supply. As Vic Szafranski said, Jack had more shit than a Christmas goose.

Though Jack may have been a consummate liar, he sure had been around. Five of us, with Jack in charge, were on our way to Detroit by car during the winter of 1949–50. There was a big snowstorm in northern Arizona and New Mexico and into the plains states. Instead of following our regular route through Flagstaff and Albuquerque, we stayed south and went through Phoenix and Tucson to Las Cruces. Once we were that far down, Jack decided that we ought to go to El Paso. At some time during the thirties, the Old Man—before the state of Texas screwed him out of a lot of money—ran his caravans all the way across Texas, from Texarkana to El Paso. Jack thought that he still might be acquainted there, and wanted to see if he could stir up some of his old cronies.

In the evening we went across the river to Juarez, fought off the kids who were trying to sell us souvenirs and their sisters, and made the rounds of the bars, having a beer in each one. In the fourth or fifth place a big guy with a craggy face stared at us for a few minutes, then came over to our table and said, "Aren't you Jack Blue?" Jack did a double take, and said, "Aren't you So-and-so?" And the guy said he sure was, and he hadn't seen Jack since they were in the China Marines together in Tsingtao. They yelled and beat each other on the back and ordered plenty more beer. They reminisced for an hour about all the wild crazy drunken rotten things they'd done together in China, and then the big guy said he knew where there was the best French Show in town. He took us to a place that had a room about ten feet wide and twenty feet long, a third of which had been made into a raised stage. All the seats were choice seats. Three Mexican girls, one with a long, hard-rubber penis strapped around her hips, put on an imaginative, energetic show, while the six of us whooped and stomped our feet and beat our hands together and drank a lot more beer. Jack said he was mighty intrigued by the one wearing the peccadillo, and Vic said it was a dildo, and Jim said what's the difference?

We thanked Jack's friend profusely, and declared that show the finest thing to come down the road since Adam and Eve.

Texas is even worse when you're hung-over, and we swore never to do it again. The Old Man was death on drinkers. He must have been desperate for a convoy leader when he took on Jack, because he'd had trouble with Jack's drinking before the war. In fact, he'd had trouble with most everyone drinking: alcohol was the universal downfall. The nature of the job, its appeal to those with the traveling fever or a drifter psychology, guaranteed that the Old Man would get more than his share of boozers.

It was a job made to order for truck-bums—men who were good drivers and reliable employees when sober, but who never stayed on a job for long. Sooner or later the whiskey would get them and they'd blow the works, or they'd get an itchy foot and move on. There was no way for the Old Man to upgrade the job and attract stable men. To do that he would have had to raise wages to the level paid on union jobs; to raise wages he'd have to increase his tariff; increasing the tariff would make him less competitive; and he felt, rightly or not, that the big unionized outfits would squeeze him out of business if he charged as much as they did.

So he kept the tariff down, cut costs wherever he could, paid substandard wages—and got what he paid for. What the Old Man wanted were drivers who were sober, married, had homes, and saved their money. What he got were lushes, eccentrics, divorced and separated men, wastrels, and spendthrifts. And somehow, the Old Man couldn't understand how that was. Every six months or so he would ask me, in a querulous or despairing tone, why he couldn't manage to attract men of a higher caliber. It was like asking how come water doesn't flow uphill—it's just how things *are.* The people who are close to the bottom have to work somewhere, and if you're offering a bottom kind of job then they'll gravitate to you. Not that those men were the scum of the Earth. They were driving for the Old Man because the nomadic life appealed to them, and because if you don't have any home territory to defend then being a nomad makes just as good sense as staying in one place.

Never Cut Your Pleasure Short

Vice . . . is a creature of such heejous mien . . . That
th' more ye see of it th' betther ye like it,
The Crusade Against Vice
Mr. Dooley (Finley Peter Dunne)

Jack was on a nostalgia kick, and was always trying to locate people he'd known before the war. He found a surprising number of them—people who were still in the same places and doing the same jobs that they'd done nine or ten years earlier. Perhaps ten years doesn't seem like such a terribly long time, but the war was a great watershed. The country was different on the other side: the passage of a decade had the effect of an entire generation gone by. The ways of thinking and of doing things had changed so much that the Old Man's operation was an anachronism—an odd, out-of-place holdover from the hard times of the thirties. Whenever Jack was recognized by someone he'd known before the war, he'd be greeted as though he'd risen from the dead—or as a latter-day Rip Van Winkle, just returned from a long sojourn in a far and foreign country.

Our route took us across the Mississippi River at Quincy, Illinois, but Jack said that there was a better road a bit farther south—a route that the Old Man had occasionally used in the thirties. One day in March 1950, Jack led us down to Springfield, and then west on U.S. 36 through Jacksonville and Pittsfield. We ran into one of the freezing rains that are so common in that part of the country, and we barely made it across the river into Hannibal, Missouri. Jack said that we would stay there because the roads weren't safe, and though the ice melted a couple of hours later, Jack wasn't interested in leaving town. He'd met a bar owner he'd once known, and they were well along on a grand reunion, consisting of heavy drinking and untrue stories beginning with "Do you remember . . . ."

It was plain to see that Jack wouldn't be in any shape to make an early start in the morning, so Vic and Jim and I set out to explore

Hannibal's potential for entertainment. We passed up such tourist traps as Becky Thatcher's cottage and Tom Sawyer's cave, rejected the movie theater, which was showing a couple of third-rate war pictures, and were obliged to settle for a night of drinking—probably what we wanted to do anyway. We made the rounds, couldn't stir up any excitement, and parked ourselves in a tavern a block from our hotel. Beer was cheap in Missouri then: twenty cents a bottle for the local brews such as Stag or Griesedieck (gimme a greasydick). Vic and Jim were experienced drinkers, and I had to work hard to keep up with them. They were at the prime time of life for drinking—old enough to have learned how to pour it down, but not so old that they couldn't handle it any more.

Along about closing time Jim asked the bartender where we could find some girls or a blind pig or both. The bartender had us figured as being okay even though we were from out of town, and he directed us two blocks this way and then two and a half blocks that way down toward the river, and there in the middle of the block was an unlit doorway with a Bell Telephone sign over it. And that was it—just go right in.

We followed his directions, located the sign, and went right in. And when we closed the door behind us it was darker in there than the bottom of a coal mine at midnight during an eclipse of the moon. We stuck out our hands, and could feel that we were in a hallway with stairs running up one side. We blundered along to the end of the hallway, where we bumped into a door. While we were debating, in noisy whispers, whether we should knock on the door or try the stairs, the door was abruptly flung open from the inside. There was a blaze of light, and framed in the doorway was a woman about four feet ten and weighing maybe 220 pounds.

"Whaddya want?" she asked in a rasping, hostile voice, and Jim said Oscar the bartender sent us and was this the place? She mellowed right away, and said to come on in and take a load off, and the girls would be down in a minute. She looked more like Tony Galento than the White Rock Sparkling maiden, so we were relieved to learn that she wasn't one of the girls. But what the hell if she had been? We were as one with Mark Twain—willing to try anything once, and some things more often.

There was a round table in the center of the room. The madam asked what we wanted to drink—she was serving beer at fifty cents a bottle and whiskey at fifty cents a shot. That sounded fair enough, so all three of us ordered whiskey and beer both. If you're going in for high living, there's no point in pulling your punches.

Two girls showed up immediately. Both were in their early twenties, dressed in skimpy cotton pants and bras—colorful, patterned material that would have been more appropriately used for kitchen curtains or tablecloths. One of the girls was medium height, medium weight, medium looks—not bad, but nothing to write home to mom about. The other looked as though she'd been eating too many potatoes. She was short and dumpy—might have been the madam's daughter—and weighed a good 200 pounds on the hoof. Her flabby flesh was falling out all over her garments. Not a very appetizing sight—good thing we'd been drinking.

In keeping with our appointed role as big spenders, we bought drinks for both girls—and for the madam, too. The madam was sure making money every way you could think of, but she was in business and we weren't and she had certain commodities for sale and we wanted to buy: the epitome of the Capitalist ethic—but I don't know if Socialism is any different.

We all sat around the table, and sipped our drinks and made small talk. Now small talk in a situation like that is so small that it almost vanishes.

"Where you boys from?"

"Nice little town you've got here."

"Goin' clear to California? That's a long ways."

"If we had some friendly company along it might be more of a pleasure."

"Well, never cut your pleasure short, that's what I always say."

We'd had at least a dozen beers apiece before we got there, and were feeling no pain. Following the example of my mentors, I tossed my whiskey down at one gulp, and I was about halfway through my beer when I felt an awful churning in my stomach and a rising wave of nausea. I politely asked the madam where was the men's room, and she said it's right over there and it's for both and where do you think you are, the Ritz-Carlton? I made it in time, locked the door behind me, and vomited for five minutes. While I was splashing water on my face and regaining my composure, I heard the fat girl ask, "Say, whatever happened to Pete?" Vic said I was in the head, and the other girl sniggered and said I was probably pissing a good hard-on away. That made me kind of mad. I rather she'd said I was sick.

When I came out, the girls and the madam looked pretty disgusted with me because I obviously wasn't going to be worth much—no profit there. But the madam was a philosophical sort, and when I ordered another beer she gave me a five-cent bag of pretzels to help settle my stomach. After a bit more empty chitchat and another round of drinks, the beef trust got impatient. She wasn't much of a hand at small talk—that is, she didn't have any—and just sitting there like a blob was more than she could stand. Suddenly she busted out and said, in a petulant voice, "Doesn't anybody wanta *fuck?*"

Vic said that he did, so he took the other girl and went upstairs. I was all set to get out of that place, but I wasn't sure how to go about it, and thought that I should take my cue from Jim. Actually, I was concerned about etiquette: I couldn't just leap up and walk out—it wasn't polite—what would people think?

Jim took a long pull on his beer bottle, said "Ah, fuck it!" and stood up. I stood up too, and out we went, with the fat whore making nasty remarks behind us. "Pisspoor excuse for men you are—can't even get it up any more." The madam wasn't happy about it, but it happened all the time and what could you do?

The next morning we asked Vic how was it, and he said well, it was all right. The girl had told him that for nine or ten months out of the year she worked in Quincy as a telephone operator. The rest of the time she spent down in Hannibal, peddling her ass, which was the way to really make the money but no girl in her right mind wanted to do that all the time. You can't fight logic like that.

In the morning when we saw Jack we asked him where he'd got to the night before, but he just gave us a big wink and a knowing grin. We weren't so reticent, and told him in detail about our night. He was highly amused to hear about the Bell Telephone sign, and told us that before the war you looked for the Coca-Cola sign. Anyplace in that whole town, if you saw a Coca-Cola sign hanging above a doorway or in front of a building that obviously wasn't a place of business—that's where the girls were. Jack was pleased to hear that they still had a system. Old Ma Bell making a little money on the side.

Goodbye, Tootsie

Not drunk is he who from the floor
Can rise alone and still drink more;
But drunk is he who prostrate lies,
Without the power to drink or rise.
The Misfortunes of Elphin
Thomas Love Peacock

Making money on the side was something I never did, although there were opportunities. If I had occasion to gas up a convoy at other than one of our regular stops, I would usually be asked how much I wanted the receipt made out for. When I'd say just for the correct amount, they'd look at me as if I wasn't all there. The practice of padding fuel and repair bills was so widespread that no one thought anything of it. Everyone figured that his boss was making money out of his employees' hides, and that padding the bills was a way of getting back a little of what was rightfully yours. But if you worked for the Old Man you realized that there was no way to get even, so if you didn't like it you should pick up your marbles and go somewhere else.

Jack said that in the thirties the caravan leaders could make as much on the side as the Old Man paid in wages. You could work up deals with hotel operators and café owners to get a kickback of so much per head if you would consistently bring your twenty or more drivers to their establishments. But those days were gone forever. The convoys were small, it was doubtful that anyone would make that sort of a deal in good times, and it was nearly impossible to cheat the Old Man even if you were so inclined. He'd been over the road so many times himself that he knew what everything cost. If he thought you'd been overcharged a tenth of a cent a gallon on gas, he was likely as not to give you the receipt and tell you to get it adjusted the next time through. That Old Man could squeeze a nickel so hard that the Indian turned blue in the face and the buffalo dropped a load.

Another old-timer who came back on the road for a spell was a man named Rummel, and of course he was called Rummy. He had been a rummy at one time, but he had gone on the wagon for good and was addicted only to cream soda. Rummy looked, talked, and acted so much like Jack that you would have thought they were twins. Rummy gave us the tales, the mystique, and the mythology of half a lifetime on the road, the confused impressions and half-remembered names and incidents—everything mixed together and disgorged in kaleidoscopic fragments, as if the details of his life were so badly scattered that they couldn't be collected and made whole again. Nor did it seem to matter. A story told one way today could be told another way tomorrow, and both versions would be equally valid. The truth of a story about the glorious dead days lay not in the accuracy of its details, but in how the storyteller, for his own salvation, chose to think about himself and his times, and it lay in how his listeners understood those times and the people who inhabited the country then. It was better to describe victories than defeats, better to think of the ludicrous than the sordid, better to remember giants than pygmies.

Rummy made four or five trips, then disappeared. He and the other old-timers were too used to the freewheeling days they remembered from before the war, and they felt cramped by the way the Old Man operated in the fifties. A couple of years later the Old Man had a letter from Rummy. He had been towbarring used cars around the country for some dealers, and had been badly injured in an accident. He was in the Veterans Administration Hospital in Grand Junction, Colorado, had been there for six months, and hadn't had a visitor in all that time. He just wanted us to know where he was, so in case anybody happened to pass that way they might stop in to see him. Grand Junction was too far from our regular route, and no one ever did get there. We never heard from Rummy again.

Bill Buschbacher came back on the job for half a dozen trips. He was about forty-five years old in 1950, and had been running a convoy when the state of Texas screwed the Old Man out of a lot of money. Buschbacher was big enough to go bear-hunting with a switch: about six foot six, with shoulders so broad that he had to order his shirts from a specialty haberdasher in New York—or so he said. Those old-timers always laid it on with a trowel.

Bush was the heaviest-footed driver I ever met. He wanted to go full blast—run the convoy until you were too tired to go any farther. For about ten trips in 1951 and 1952 we drove back to Detroit in the Old Man's car, and towed the car back out to L.A. behind whatever we were transporting. The Old Man had a 1951 Hudson Super-Six with overdrive, one of the best road cars ever built. One time when we went east in that car, with Bush in charge, we drove right straight through. For the sake of variety we stayed on U.S. 66 to Springfield, Illinois. From Tulsa to Detroit no one passed us. I woke up once when we were in northeast Illinois on U.S. 54, a good straight-arrow highway, and Bush was driving a flat ninety-five. That was with six men in the car, a trunk full of towbars, and a pile of suitcases on the luggage rack. If we'd blown a tire at that speed we'd still be out there, knocking down corn stalks.

Bush left the job late in 1951, and got onto the Indio police force as a detective. Now and again we'd see him in Indio when we passed through with a convoy; he'd be charging around town at sixty miles an hour in second gear. Later on he too was in a bad accident, and suffered a broken back. When he was healed he left Indio, and we never heard of him again either.

The Old Man's brother Carl made three trips on Divcos. He was like the Old Man in being businesslike and pinchpenny on the job, but he also liked to have a laugh, and he was freehanded with his own money. Breakdowns and bad weather didn't bother him at all. He treated them as humorous incidents, the raw material for future tall tales that would widen the eyes of newcomers in the years ahead. In the early thirties Carl ran caravans of Auburns to L.A. and Seattle. He delighted in telling about the time, in the dead of winter, that a series of snowstorms delayed a caravan so badly that after three weeks of heroic effort it was hopelessly bogged down north of Cedar City, Utah. The Old Man loaded a car with chains and ropes, and came up from L.A. to the rescue. The entire trip took thirty-two days. In those days, Carl said, U.S. 30 was unpaved west of Sidney, Nebraska. But that's almost before the dawn of time—an era alive only in the memories of a vanishing race.

Carl's health was failing, and he had to get off the road. He died a year later.

Jack lasted for a year and a half, off and on. He'd be strictly business for a couple of trips, but then he'd start drinking and the Old Man would get wind of it and give him his walking papers. In a month or two it would all be forgiven and Jack would be back driving again. He'd shun that fatal first glass of beer. When the rest of us went out to have a few before turning in for the night, Jack would stay in his hotel room reading detective magazines and looking at the pictures in the *Police Gazette.*

The information he gathered from those sources accorded perfectly with his view of what people were like and what life was all about. All that was missing were some good stories about towbarring.

In January 1951 we were stuck for two days in Grants, New Mexico, by a blizzard and cold wave. This was before the big uranium strike in northwest New Mexico transformed Grants into a boom town. Its population in 1951 was less than a thousand, and the only way the people could stay alive was to milk the tourists. The town consisted mainly of decrepit, crumbling adobe houses, with gas stations and shabby motels along U.S. 66 through the middle of town. If it hadn't been for the highway and the railroad, the town would have blown away.

We holed up in the poshest spot in town—The Yucca Hotel, with café, bar, and Greyhound bus station all under one roof. The hotel had the smallest rooms I ever saw—about the size of a monk's cell. One of the drivers said that his room was so small that the bed was painted on the wall, and he had to sleep standing up. Jack held out the first day, but on the second he fell off the wagon with a bang. We provided Grants' night-life—beginning at lunch—and by evening Jack had about three sheets in the wind.

This was the time when Al Jolson was enjoying a big revival: his records were on every jukebox in the country. Hearing all those old songs made Jack sentimental, and when Jolson sang "Toot toot tootsie, goodbye, Toot toot tootsie, don't cry," Jack started to cry. Big tears came rolling down his cheeks and splashed onto the bar. He got up off his stool, went out in the middle of the floor, and did a soft-shoe dance in time to the music while he sang along with good old Al, but he was blubbering so much you couldn't make out the words. Jack noticed our astonishment even though he was overwhelmed by nostalgia, emotion, and alcohol, and he managed to give us a wink and a grin through the tears. When the record ended, Jack pulled out his big red-checked handkerchief, snorted hard into it, and ordered another shot with a beer chaser. Whenever things got slow, somebody would drop a nickel in and punch the button for "Toot toot tootsie, goodbye." It never failed. A dozen times that night Jack got up and did his dance, bawling like a baby all the while.

That was the last trip Jack made. He couldn't stay off the sauce, and there was no way to flummox the Old Man. Being near Jack was like being downwind from a distillery. The Old Man canned Jack for good, and he was gone too.

“If you don’t get a letter
Then you’ll know I’m in jail.”

Solidarity Forever

> To protect the workers in their inalienable rights to a higher and better life; to protect them, not only as equals before the law, but also in their health, their homes, their firesides, their liberties as men, as workers, and as citizens; to overcome and conquer prejudices and antagonism; to secure to them the right to life, and the opportunity to maintain that life; the right to be full sharers in the abundance which is the result of their brain and brawn, and the civilization of which they are the founders and the mainstay; to this the workers are entitled . . . . The attainment of these is the glorious mission of the trade unions.
>
> ***From a speech in 1898***
> **Samuel Gompers**

By the end of 1949 I had made ten trips. The Old Man decided that I was going to be around for a spell, and had me fill out an application for employment. Early in 1950, at the age of twenty-one, I became a convoy leader, a position of responsibility that I had neither expected nor sought. It was a logical move for the Old Man to make, even though I was the youngest man on the job. The old-timers were too erratic, Vic and Jim gave indications that they wouldn't stick for long, and thus I was chosen by default. Had the Old Man been able to foretell the future, he would have dropped me at once. When the end came, the Old Man blamed me for killing his business.

But the Old Man, like most people, was stumbling backward into the future with his eyes fixed on the past. He was as firmly in the clutches of his habits and his memories as were Jack Blue and Rummy and the others from before the war—a man out of his time, doing things the way he'd always done them, running on momentum, putting in his days on the way to the end.

When the Old Man saw that he could make a decent profit transporting Divcos, he loosened his grip on the money. He stopped deducting hotel expenses from our paychecks, and paid the bills himself. He raised our wages to $112.50 per trip, a princely sum compared to what it was at the beginning but miserly compared to what drivers were getting on union jobs. A full round trip took two weeks—ten days going out, at least a day in Los Angeles, two days back to Detroit on the train, and a day or two in Detroit getting ready to go again. At that rate we were doing well to make two round trips a month—10,000 miles of travel for $225.

But we didn't feel like victims unless we dwelled upon our minor grievances. We were on the road because we wanted to be. We were driving for the Old Man because we had stumbled onto the job, and there was something so satisfying about it that the drawbacks were of little consequence. There were no obvious tangible benefits, no visible rewards that could be deposited in the bank or hung on the wall or worn like a suit of new clothes or converted into society's esteem. Yet we went back and forth, squandering the most alert hours of our best years—and though we may not have been ecstatic, we were not unhappy.

I came to feel that a man's most important undertaking in life is to go out and see the land, and that's what the Old Man's job was good for. If there was social value hidden in what we were doing, it was private and personal—kept us out of the poolhalls while keeping us in walking-around money. Herding Divcos across the country was work for drifters, which to our way of thinking made it better than work that paid the top dollar but tied you down. An inquisitive tourist once asked Jim what a Divco was worth, and Jim replied that he wouldn't give a fiddler's fuck for all the Divcos in the world. But the true value of Divcos was the very fact of their existence: because they existed, we could go traveling.

Some of the great satisfactions on the job were the recurring ones. Between Las Animas and La Junta, I was always pleased anew when, on a clear day, I could see the blue misty bulk of Pike's Peak on the horizon. In the spring, it was good to see yellow blossoms on the creosote bushes along the highway from Blythe to Indio. Going south from Raton I was always eager for the first glimpse of Wagon Mound. I would be amused once again by the pretentious legend "Where the Prairie Begins" painted on the east side of a barn outside Wolcott, Indiana. And every time that I crossed the Missouri River at Leavenworth I felt that I had broken loose from the old, tired part of the country, and was going into virgin territory.

There was much about the job that was not to our liking, and we kept nibbling away at it, smoothing out the rough edges, improving our lot. After I led my third convoy, I approached the Old Man, with considerable trepidation, and put it up to him that we did not care in the least for doubling-up in hotel beds. As was his custom, and instinct, the Old Man balked at making any change that would cost him money, as though such a suggestion was tantamount to tapping his bloodstream —as perhaps it was. The Old Man would not give in to direct pressure. You had to put objections into a context that made economic sense, or figure out how to embarrass him: make him regard what he was doing as cheap and despicable rather than sensibly frugal.

Not that I was so clever as to discern the Old Man's biases and turn them to our advantage, or that he had a glass head and I could see the wheels go around. Whereas the Old Man's instinct was automatic resistance to costly change—any cost at all—my instinct was to put complaints and proposals for change in terms of moral outrage, mildly expressed but unmistakable, or by pointing out to him that he obliged us to do what he would not do himself. In the matter of doubling-up, there was no problem. The Old Man's reaction was typical: silence, and an unblinking stare, as though an extreme request had aroused him to such anger that he could control himself only by not uttering a word or moving a muscle. You had merely to wait, staring back or casually looking aside, and in under a minute the Old Man would give you his answer. It was fatal to your position to be disconcerted by the Old Man's initial lack of response, and to feel that the chilly silence must be overcome by your own babbling. Invariably you undercut your argument, and made it easy for the Old Man to turn you down. The one thing he was good at was detecting someone else's weakness.

We felt pretty good about getting beds to ourselves, which simply demonstrates that everything is relative. Under no circumstances had any of us tolerated such a thing before, nor could we imagine that we would hold still for that sort of treatment in the future. Even the army let you sleep in your own bunk.

But the Old Man had a psychology of scarcity. He ran his business as though the wolf was at the door, and if a few more pennies slipped through his fingers he'd get shipped out to the poor farm. There was constant pressure from the Old Man to economize, to do things in whatever way saved visible expense even though there was great cost in human effort and discomfort. Staying in worn-out country hotels, buying cut-rate gas, and sleeping two in a bed got to us after a while, and without knowing what had happened to us we acquired some of the Old Man's attitudes. A cheapjack operation seemed justified by necessity, and if we lived as though poverty-stricken it was not because we were underpaid, but rather was due to the poverty-stricken aura created by the Old Man. We could have been in the midst of the greatest boom ever, yet the Old Man would have been scraping along like that hillbilly on the first trip: beans and bread, bread and beans, and never a bite of steak. Somebody said that the Old Man had the first dollar he'd ever made, framed and under glass, hanging over the mantel.

I had been brought up to save money, not throw it around, and I found it natural and easy to send every third paycheck to the savings and loan for deposit. I wasn't saving for any particular purpose or because I was more virtuous: it was entirely the result of early training. With few exceptions, the others had no idea of what to do with their money other than to spend it, and they were prone to run through their cash as if it were going out of style. Being broke was endemic, and blame for those always empty pockets was chronically attributed to the Old Man's skinflint wages. A prevalent notion was that if the Old Man were to pay the going wage for towbar work, everybody would have money to burn, but there was no evidence to substantiate that. Those guys who drove for the Old Man were talented: they could spend money faster than the government could print it.

But still, there was the nebulous idea that a union wage would be our salvation, an idea engendered by the three-dollar trip fee, deducted from our paychecks by the Old Man, that we paid to the Teamsters Union. Jim Baumann confessed to having a union card from a local in California, but he was out on withdrawal and wasn't about to tell them that he was working on a non-union job for fear they'd hang him by the balls.

Vic and I learned that the union's initiation fee was thirty-two dollars. When we had made enough trips, at three dollars a trip, to cover the fee, we decided to get membership cards. Paying four dollars a month dues was a bit cheaper than three dollars a trip, if we were working steady, but the main reason for joining the union was our hope that union cards would grease the way to union wages and union benefits. We had no intention of putting the skids under the Old Man, but in our innocence, and ignorance of the economics involved, we thought that it would be a simple matter to erase this discrepancy, this little oversight on the part of the union. As the punch line to that old talking blues has it: "Take it easy, but *take* it." Yeah—well, we wanted some.

If you were working out of Detroit on a haulaway or driveaway job, you were a member of Local 299, Jimmy Hoffa's home local—unless you worked for the Old Man. The union hall was near downtown, on Trumbull Avenue. When we got there Vic remarked that there were more Cadillacs in the union's parking lot than there were at the Cadillac factory.

For reasons that we couldn't decipher we were treated like lepers who spoke an incomprehensible language. We insisted that we wanted to become members, that our accumulated trip fees were sufficient to cover the initiation, that the Old Man mailed in our trip fees every month, and that all they need do was to look up our records. For an hour we were shuffled from one office to another, and were variously informed that there was no such thing as a trip fee, they had never heard of the Old Man, all driveaway jobs were already unionized, they had no records of us or our presumed payments, the initiation fee was cash on the barrelhead, and we were out of our skulls.

All the answers were negative, and had I been alone I would have been defeated. Vic was more determined: he said that he'd paid good money into that place and byjesus he was going to find out what had happened to it or he'd raise Hail Columbia. Logically what should have happened at that point was that they'd call the goon squad and give us the bum's rush. But someone of greater knowledge and authority apparently got wind of what was going on, and, to our astonishment, we suddenly were given the red-carpet treatment. They found our records after all, by golly, and would fix us up in no time.

We were ushered into the office of Frank Collins, Secretary-Treasurer of the local, the man second in command to Hoffa. Collins was all sweetness and light, and said of course he knew the Old Man and how was the old gent getting along? We said that he was making it okay, but we were more concerned about ourselves. Collins said that was right and you had to look out for Number One, but how come we wanted to join the union? We told him the truth: it was cheaper to pay monthly dues than a trip fee, and maybe, just maybe, a membership card would lead to higher wages and better working conditions. If we were members, wouldn't the union see to it that we got a fair deal? Collins didn't believe a word we said: he suspected something more subtle and, it seemed, dangerous. He said that the only way for us to get union benefits was if the Old Man signed a union contract, but what he wanted to know was why we *really* wanted to become members. We kept giving him the same answers, and we were mystified when he didn't believe us. Collins was all smiles right to the end. He finally issued membership cards and signed our dues books, and we went back out into the real world, not at all certain what we had achieved.

The next trip out, we showed our cards and dues books to the Old Man so that he would stop deducting the trip fee. The Old Man became as jittery and suspicious as Collins had been. One of the dirtier words in the Old Man's lexicon was *union*. Perhaps he was afraid that we were going to try to organize him, which would have put the kibosh on his whole operation and run him out of business. I managed to convince him that all we were after was not to have to pay so much to the union, and also it would give us the opportunity to get a union job. When the Old Man could see that we weren't going to do him in, he explained what the trip fee was all about.

The union initiated trip fees in 1942 as a temporary wartime measure. School teachers, office workers, and others who were working a straight five-day week, were hired to drive new army trucks from Detroit and Flint to the boat docks at Philadelphia, Baltimore, and Brooklyn. They would leave Friday afternoon, and be back home Sunday night or Monday morning. They weren't regular union members, and the trip fee was the union's way of retaining control. Trip fees were abolished after the war; there was a section in the union's constitution saying that they were illegal.

The Old Man had never been unionized, and wasn't about to be; he'd sooner see the world come to an end. But the union wasn't going to let the Old Man off scot-free. According to the Old Man, he and Hoffa had lunch one day in Detroit. He paid off Hoffa under the table, and agreed to give the union three dollars per man per trip as the price of untroubled operation. Hoffa didn't care where the money came from; he just wanted it. The Old Man hit on the idea of taking it out of his employees' pay, because he didn't care where it came from either—just so long as it wasn't out of his pocket.

That made it clear; we were being sandbagged, and now we knew how, why, and by whom. Had we complained to the union they would have given us a swift kick, and if we had refused to let the Old Man deduct the three dollars he would have told us to take a hike—there were plenty of other guys ready to go on the road. You could have put the Old Man and Hoffa on the witness stand, and each would have sworn, in all sincerity, that the other was guilty. And they both would have been right. It is axiomatic that it takes at least two crooks to make one crooked deal.

We had no great desire for a union, and if the Old Man had had his wits about him we never would have thought about a union. We didn't want to stick it in the Old Man's ribs or to shut down his business, nor did we want to become the victims of a crooked union in order to milk the Old Man for a higher wage. All we wanted were working conditions that were comfortable at best and bearable at worst, and enough cash to buy the necessaries of life and a few of the luxuries, with something left over for a good time.

By the Rivers of Babylon

> It is my belief, Watson, founded upon long experience, that the lowest and vilest alleys of London do not present a more dreadful record of sin than does the smiling and beautiful countryside.
>
> *The Adventures of Sherlock Holmes*
> **Sir Arthur Conan Doyle**

Quincy, Illinois and Albuquerque, New Mexico were the biggest towns we went through on the entire route. In 1950 both had populations of about 40,000, but Quincy had enough action for a town three times its size. With a little money and a little carelessness a man could get laid, relaid, and waylaid all in an evening.

The various forms of vice were illegal in Quincy, but minor-league gambling and prostitution flourished openly. Restaurants and bars usually had slot machines tucked away in back rooms or dark corners, placed so that you would pass them going to the restroom. Every eating and drinking place, hotel desk, market, drug store, and service station had punch boards, which was true of the entire state.

Quincy had so much cheap prostitution that the local girls had been forced into giving it away, meaning that their ministrations were free but out of pride they wanted a guy with a big shiny car to spend money on them—which automatically disqualified anyone working for the Old Man. It was sometimes embarrassing, because the free girls and the ones for hire looked and dressed pretty much alike, and both classes tended to feel insulted if mistaken for the other.

Third Street in Quincy, three blocks up the hill from the river, had the sort of notoriety to attract traveling salesmen, farm boys, truck drivers, and others of the wayfaring and excitable breed. One warm evening in the spring of 1950, Vic and Jim and I took a stroll down Third Street to see if the reputation was well earned. There was no mistake: twice, girls in second-story windows attracted our attention by throwing pebbles at us. In a three-block stretch there were eight taverns, each with blinking colored lights, a squall of fiddles and nasal singing from a jukebox, and a lonesome girl or two sitting at the bar and staring expectantly at the door. There were three establishments with big picture windows. The girls sat next to the windows, wearing pants and bras made from print material that looked like old flour sacks, knitting and creaking back and forth in rocking chairs. When we walked by they clicked their fingernails on the glass and gave us the high sign. A girl standing in a doorway said that she'd like to give us something we'd never had before, and Vic wanted to know if she had the Chinese crud. Her answer showed that she was no lady.

One of the picture-window places was diagonally across the street from the police station, which showed that the cops weren't gentlemen. As we sauntered by the place, a girl came out on the sidewalk and gave us a warm invite to step inside her lair for a little party. She even tried to entice us with an offer of coffee and cookies to get things off on the right foot. Jim thought that was a mighty peculiar ploy, and it made him suspicious about what other oddball things might be going on in there, so he declined to play and said he'd mosey on down the street. The girl got huffy and asked Jim if he was too cheap, and Jim said that he was saving himself so he'd have something to play with in his old age.

Vic and I let the girl drag us inside, and after a bit of dickering Vic, who was always game for anything, went upstairs with the girl, leaving me to cope with another one. She started out asking five dollars for a little short-time, and came all the way down to two dollars for around-the-world. To hear her tell about the aged grandmother she was supporting was enough to melt stone, and made me think that perhaps I should buy her wares just to be a Good Samaritan. But I fought down that impulse and respectfully declined to support her grandmother on the grounds that I had a noble and faithful wife whose memory I would not care to besmirch, whereupon that wheedling whore turned into a screech owl and yelled at me to get my ass out of that place, which I did with alacrity. When I saw Vic an hour or so later he was stunned at the low price I'd been quoted, and disgusted with me because I'd let the opportunity slip by. He said that even if I didn't want any I should have taken it because that was a bargain-basement special, and even if it had been bad it would have been good. It had cost him a fin, which he had thought a rock-bottom price, to get screwed, blewed, and tattooed, and it rankled him that I'd let a live one get away. He didn't think I'd had proper fetching up.

All the drivers who had knocked around a lot said that Quincy had a fair amount of life, but that for a really wild town you should go to Steubenville, Ohio; Hurley, Wisconsin; Covington, Kentucky; and any town in Missouri big enough to have a tavern. A couple of local boys overheard us talking, said they thought Quincy was fairly tame, and that when they were out for excitement they always went to Beardstown, sixty miles east of Quincy on the Illinois River, which was guaranteed to be a couple of notches ahead of Sodom and Gomorrah. This created certain longings in some of the Old Man's drivers, since our route took us right past Beardstown but chances were slim that we would ever hit Sodom and Gomorrah.

A year and a half later, with a convoy of eight hookups of taxicabs, we were snowed in at Beardstown for two nights. Vic and Jim had long since left the job, but the mythology of driving for the Old Man had been passed on to their successors, and the reputation of Beardstown had become enhanced in the passage. Beardstown was known, or had been known, as Little Reno on the River. That title conjured up visions of wanton activity, and aroused great anticipation in the crew. By the time we had parked the taxis and checked into the hotel, everyone was ready for assault, rapine, lewd and lascivious behavior, dipsomania, and whatever other delights Beardstown might offer.

It was a dark and stormy night in the wilds of Illinois, and there wasn't a bacchanalia in sight. Beardstown's heyday was past, leaving the usual residue of inflamed memories and the exaggerations of old gaffers. We tried every tavern in town, walked expectantly down dark streets until our feet were wet and cold from the snow, and had our senses honed for the least sign of sin and corruption, but nothing of interest came within our purview. It surpassed comprehension. Beardstown had, for our purposes, died, and been buried standing. Word of the funeral had not reached us, and we suspected chicanery. But the truth, when we knew it, was clear and guileless: sin and corruption had been subverted by politics. Adlai Stevenson was elected governor in 1948, and had done much to clean up the state.

Most of the drivers, both the steady men and the one-ways, were broke most of the time. A convoy leader's regular practice was to advance each driver three dollars a day, enough for a man to have three squares and buy some smokes. When we were delayed by bad weather or a breakdown, I upped the ante to five dollars a head to relieve the tedium of sitting around all day with nothing to do. If you were willing to eat lightly, you could do enough drinking on that five dollars to become mellow. The least fortunate circumstance, from the pilot's point of view, was for a driver to be beset by a drinking problem and to have his advance in his pocket and time on his hands.

Max Jankel was such a case on the trip when we stayed in Beardstown. Max was a journeyman carpenter. He made a trip as a one-way driver, saying that he had lined up a job in Alaska, and that getting to the Coast was the first leg of the journey. But in Los Angeles he got drunk and missed out on the job, so he made more trips. Each trip was to be his last, and he would then go on to Alaska. Each trip he blew his pay on booze, and when broke and sober decided to make another trip for the Old Man.

Max was a large, hulking man, polite in speech, benign in attitude, gentle and friendly. Even when soused he did not become belligerent or boisterous. He became less inhibited, but still behaved so calmly that you didn't realize that the barriers were down until he gently and politely committed an untoward act.

In Beardstown, Max neglected to eat. He spent all his advance on beer, managing to be drunk for the first twenty-four hours. In midafternoon of the second day Max found me in a café, and hit me up for another advance—which he did every time he saw me. I was reduced to giving him fifty cents at a crack, with the stipulation that if he spent it then and there on food and coffee, I would give him another fifty cents to spend as he pleased. Max, without appetite, was dutifully mashing a piece of pie to a pulp with his fork, when he felt the need to go the restroom. The café had but one restroom, and when Max tried the door he couldn't get it open—because the woman who owned the café was in there, sitting on the pot, and of course she had the door hooked. But Max was desperate, and was not to be deterred. He jerked at the door with ever-increasing strength, and finally tore it open with a mighty heave, ripping out the hook and splintering the door jamb.

Max peered in, the woman glared out, but it was Max's inning and he was in full control. He reached in, gently patted the woman on the head, and politely closed the door. The customers and waitresses went into hysterics. Max beamed warmly, pleased that he was the cause of so much mirth. The woman broke the transcontinental record for getting her britches up, and stormed out with fire in her eye, the desire to commit mayhem, and terrible threats of a lifetime at hard labor for Max. I quickly gave Max his next fifty cents and sent him off to a tavern. We managed to sweet-talk the woman out of calling the law, and she settled for eighty-sixing Max for the rest of his natural life.

Deeply felt myths die hard, and the guys hit the taverns again the second night, hoping that the first had been a fluke. But reality is truth even when you don't like it, and after another night of talking to bartenders and watching the neon signs flash, they all became believers in the new gospel: Beardstown was a cemetery with lights, a haven for the old and the weary, and any normal American boy with piss and vinegar surging through his veins should get on down the road to where the good-time girls had flown.

In the morning, Ernie Jeska bragged that he had picked up a girl in a bowling alley and screwed her in the back seat of one of the taxis, but the taxis had cold imitation-leather upholstery and no heaters, and the temperature had been near zero. Although Ernie was a nice guy and no one wanted to call him an out-and-out liar, there was an air of skepticism. Ernie admitted that the girl had been a mite disgruntled when her bare ass hit the cold seat, but he swore that it was true nevertheless. Well, if Ernie wanted to believe that it had happened it was okay with us. It was the kind of story that everyone wanted to believe, and in later years even the skeptics were converted. The tale about when Ernie had knocked off a hot piece in a cold taxi became part of the standard repertoire. Through that tale the reputation of Beardstown was preserved, and in the late fifties there was some mild yearning to stay overnight in a hotspot like Beardstown rather than in the moribund whistlestops of northeast Missouri.

In midmorning of the third day Max attempted to seduce a chambermaid in the hotel corridor, which terrified the girl and brought suspicion and disgrace upon us all. Max did her no harm, since he was merely being warm and friendly after his own fashion. He put his big hands on her and smiled and exhaled his beery breath. The girl was young and lacking in experience, and she mistook these friendly gestures for an attack, and as long as we were in the hotel she refused to go upstairs and perform her duties.

Fortunately there was a break in the weather, and by late afternoon we were on our way. There was agitation to stay in Quincy, but I took the convoy fifteen miles farther to Palmyra, Missouri, a town big enough to have taverns yet so peaceful that you could have fired a cannon down the main drag at nine in the evening and not hit anyone.

By 1952 Quincy had become more genteel. There were no slots, the picture-window places had folded up, and even punchboards were scarce. Those who had made money from such enterprises and those who had spent it bemoaned the passing of better times, and unanimously blamed the demise of a robust culture on Stevenson. If there was anything that the people of Illinois hated worse than a dishonest governor, it was an honest one.

The Romance of the Road

The best you get is an even break.
Ballade of Schopenhauer's Philosophy
Franklin P. Adams

The innocent act of acquiring a union card could change your life, but not in the way you might have imagined. A union card is like a passport or an invention or a new toy. The absence of something you never had doesn't bother you, but when you hear about the existence of such a thing you begin to think about having one for your very own. After a spell it seems as though you can't live without one, so you hustle around and get it. And once you have it, it must be used. The knowledge of passports has you looking at maps and dreaming of distant countries. A passport in your pocket runs you down to the travel agent to buy a ticket.

Those who drove for the Old Man and didn't have union cards could only think fancifully about driving on a union job, making better money, salting some away, getting a cottage with a white picket fence or a big house on the hill, and having a squaw to take care of the brats who were bound to come along in season.

Vic and Jim and I had union cards, and those little pasteboard rectangles came to dominate our lives. It got so that we couldn't think about anything but getting onto a job that paid off in hard cash instead of the buttons and peanuts the Old Man gave us.

We kept our ears to the ground, and in September of 1950 we heard that Fleet Carrier, a driveaway outfit in Pontiac that transported GMC trucks, was hiring. When we were temporarily laid off by the Old Man we went to Pontiac, and they said come back tomorrow. We did that, and they had us fill out applications and said come back tomorrow. Two days later they hired all three of us, and said come back tomorrow. Every day we went back and forth between Detroit and Pontiac; every day we inched a little closer to actually working for union wages. There was an I.C.C. medical exam one day, a one-hour safety lecture the next, issuance of clearance lights, reflectors, and fusees the day after that. It took more than a week for the preliminaries, and we were plenty disgusted because we had to eat every day and all this red tape wasn't bringing in a dime.

One day they said be here at eight sharp tomorrow morning, and we'll send you out on your first trip. We were there at eight sharp and sat around all day until they said come back tomorrow. Jim said "Ah, fuck it!" and he turned in his equipment and took off for California to get a job driving semi-dump. Vic and I came back tomorrow and sat around all day until dinnertime, when they gave both of us trips to Cleveland under the supervision of one of their older drivers, but there was no point in leaving until about midnight because Cleveland was only 190 miles and we couldn't deliver the trucks until business hours.

We came back at midnight, and as we pulled away from the yard I noticed that my oil pressure gauge didn't register. I flashed my lights, we all stopped, we all looked at the gauge, and no one could figure out what was wrong. I took the trucks back to the yard. The dispatcher said that there wasn't anyone to fix it at midnight, and I should go home and come back tomorrow. I told him he'd look pretty funny going down the road with those trucks of mine sticking up his ass, and I quit.

Vic lasted about two months with Fleet Carrier. He made decent wages, but because he didn't have any seniority he got short trips to difficult places—small-town dealers in southern Ohio and Kentucky, reached over narrow winding roads, so far back in the hills that there wasn't any public transportation, and he had to hitchhike out. In late November they gave him a trip to New Jersey, and he got on the road just in time to get caught in the big Thanksgiving Day blizzard that hit Ohio and western Pennsylvania. He made it as far as Canfield, Ohio, and was stuck at a roadside diner for two days. The Pennsylvania state police wouldn't let commercial traffic into the state, and at the beginning of the third day Vic got tired of drinking coffee and playing cards. He ran his trucks into a big snowdrift behind the diner, removed the license plates and clearance lights, took the Greyhound back to Pontiac, and quit.

For Vic, being on the road was a last fling before settling down again. He got a job in a brewery, paid off the back alimony, remarried, and gained custody of the two kids from his first marriage. His second wife had a job, and together they worked their way up from scratch. Over a period of three of four years they changed cars and living quarters several times, moving up from an old clunker to a new car. And from a rundown rooming house in a decaying neighborhood to a house of their own in a semi-rural area.

Vic was one of the few who went from bad to better instead of worse. Driving for the Old Man was like being addicted to a mild narcotic: it was a debilitating habit and you couldn't kick it, although it wouldn't kill you. But neither were you going to get anywhere. Driving for the Old Man was a dead end, because you knew that the Old Man was getting on, and when he quit business or died in harness you'd be out in the cold and not any farther along to anywhere than you were when you started. For most of the Old Man's drivers, being on the road was downhill all the way. They weren't headed toward anything, but were escaping from whatever plagued their lives, which usually was a blend of woman trouble and money trouble.

The drivers who lasted longest with the Old Man were the ones whose home lives had broken down entirely. When your marriage went smash and your wife got her meathooks into you for everything you could earn, then it no longer made sense to work steady and stay in the same place. If your ex-wife had a judgment requiring you to pay her so much a month, you had to pay or she'd get the law after you. The only way to avoid being taken over the jumps was to burn all your bridges and go across some state lines. And once you had cut yourself loose, the easiest thing to do was to blow around the country like a tumbleweed. The prevailing social winds blow from east to west, so naturally you would go to Detroit to see if you could get a car to take to the Coast. If you were lucky, you'd stumble onto one of the Old Man's convoys. Maybe you would make a trip as a one-way driver, and disappear into Los Angeles. Or you would make the one-way trip, then ask to make another and be taken on because we just happened to need another steady man. It was all a matter of blind dumb luck.

Over a period of two years the Old Man gradually got away from a total dependence on Divcos. In late 1950 he transported fifty Plymouth taxis to the Yellow Cab Company in L.A., and he had taxis every year after that through 1955, from 100 to 350 a year. In the early fifties the Old Man couldn't be persuaded to dig up some truck business. He was so hooked on the idea and practice of towbarring cars and Divcos in convoys that he couldn't conceive of getting trucks and making three-way combinations with them; it just wasn't the way he did things. Nevertheless we had a few trucks—a stray Dodge, a few Ford pickups, now and then a couple of Brockways going to the Los Angeles Department of Water and Power. The volume of business was erratic:

sometimes we had none, and everybody went home for a week or two or tried to get some temporary work. At other times we were overwhelmed by taxis and Divcos, had two eight-hookup convoys on the road at the same time, and still there would be thirty or more cars sitting on the lot in Detroit when we left.

Everything about the job was erratic, unpredictable. Cars and trucks wouldn't show up on schedule or couldn't be found; the mail wouldn't get through and I wouldn't have any expense money; the mounting yard would be lax about doing the hookup work; one-way drivers would disappear before we could get on the road, and I'd have to call Kay Daley for a replacement; somebody was always drunk or hungover; and you couldn't tell what the Old Man would do next. Least of all could you tell whether all the cars would hold together. I can't understand how we ever accomplished anything. It seems only logical that the combination of persnickety vehicles, vagaries of weather, an employer who hated to spend money to make money, and a collection of drivers who were adrift in the world, should have conspired to create nothing but confusion and stagnation. How we ever did it is all a great mystery.

A greater mystery was how most of the Old Man's drivers had come to be what they were. Those in their thirties and forties had such complicated histories, related piecemeal, that you could never make sense out of the fragments or understand how their lives had gone awry. Those in their early twenties were more readily comprehended: they were footloose, wanted to see the world, and usually were just knocking around before settling down to dull lives doing some kind of work they didn't give a damn about, and inaccurately recalling the great good times driving over the road for the Old Man, staying in a different town every night, headed west with the sunlight pouring through the windshield, going out across that beautiful empty country where the wind blows for a thousand miles and the only thing to stop it is three strands of barbed wire—and that's generally down.

On my first trip as convoy leader, in the spring of 1950, I had four hookups of Divcos. Vic was along as the mechanic, and we had two one-way drivers. One of those was Steve Mikulich—nicknamed Mickey—a short, heavyset man in his late thirties, bound for L.A. to escape the snow and ice in Detroit. The first day out of Detroit we got snowed in at Coldwater, Michigan, and were stuck there for two days until the weather broke. Mickey was a fast talker. He told his life history forward and backward, and confused us completely. He had two occupations, cook and truck driver, and he had varicose veins which gave him a lot of trouble when he cooked and had to stand up all day so he'd go driving to rest his legs but all that bouncing on cold seats would make his hemorrhoids flare up and he'd have to go back to cooking. Mickey always said that if he'd been lucky enough to have been born a woman and could make his living lying down, he'd probably get bedsores.

Mickey was broke when we left Detroit, so from the beginning he was drawing against his pay. I explained the policy of advancing three dollars a night, and Mickey asked for ten dollars because he wanted to send five to his daughter in New York state and to call his sister in Detroit. I gave him the ten. Two hours later he came to my room and said that he hadn't been able to get through to his sister, and had therefore sent the whole ten to his daughter and was now flat again and needed three to eat on but how about five because he wanted to buy a cheap pair of gloves, a magazine, and a tin of Copenhagen snuff, which was his only vice. Mickey's face was red and he was talking faster than usual; I had some suspicion that his daughter resided in a bottle. But I was only twenty-one and it was my first trip as convoy leader. I wanted to believe Mickey even though I suspected that he was lying, and also I didn't have the heart to refuse money to a man who was seventeen years my senior. So I gave him the five. Later I became much more strict about advancing money, and didn't in the least mind dribbling out three dollars at a crack to full-grown men. The best way to keep all those harum-scarum drivers under control was to have them stone-broke and dependent on me for money.

To help pass the time we bought a deck of cards and played nickel-ante poker. Vic and I held good cards, and between us we split Mickey's five dollars. I advanced him five more, and we won that, too. I gave him three more to eat on, and he spent it on booze and needed another three in the morning to eat on. The trip took twelve days because of being delayed by the snow. It was a ruinous trip for Mickey. When we reached L.A. he had drawn his entire pay and was just as broke as when we'd started out. Luckily for him we had a whole herd of Divcos back in Detroit, and he signed on to make more trips. It took him a long time to catch up financially, what with sending money to his daughter —who turned out to be real—and supporting more vices than just dipping snuff.

When we left L.A. to go back to Detroit, Mickey already was drawing on the next trip's pay. He drew on that pay for five thousand miles, and when we hit L.A. again the pay was all used up. You could go on like that until they served mint juleps in hell, and if you didn't grit your teeth and spend the money slower than you made it you would never get well. For those guys who couldn't stand prosperity, and had to blow their money in as soon as they got it, working for the Old Man was like being an indentured servant with no time limit on your servitude; or like being a one-mule sharecropper whose crop was only big enough to pay off the debt to the boss but not big enough to provide seed for the next crop. I'd kid Mickey and tell him that the Old Man had him where the hair was short, and Mickey would spit a gob of that brown juice and clutch at his groin and inquire how could I be talking to him when he had me by the head.

During the first six months I worked for the Old Man we usually went back to Detroit by train. It was the best part of the job: forty-eight hours of relaxation and no responsibilities, just sleeping and reading and watching the scenery roll by. The streamliners were extra fare, so the Old Man put us aboard the Grand Canyon Limited on the Santa Fe. It was a few hours slower than the Chief or El Capitan, the day-coach seats weren't as comfortable, and we sometimes thought that it was shunted around like a cattle train, but we had no complaints. The only nuisance of the journey was changing stations in Chicago by Parmalee Transfer, and then getting on the Wolverine to Detroit. Our towbars were shipped east by truck, and the rest of our equipment was packed into several large trunks and checked through on our tickets. The sole drawback to riding the train was the added personal expense—the club car siphoned off a lot of money.

Eating was no more expensive than if we'd been driving, since the only meals we ate in the diner were two breakfasts, and in those days you could still get a good breakfast for ninety-five cents.

The first evening, about four hours out of Los Angeles, the train made a long stop at Barstow, and the passengers ate dinner in the depot cafeteria. It seemed like a relaxed, homey way to run a railroad, and it wouldn't have surprised us any if there had been a layover until morning because the engines couldn't see to drive at night. The other meals could be handled by getting food-to-go at depot lunch counters, or by getting something from the news butcher who had any kind of sandwich you wanted so long as it was ham or cheese which were sliced so thin you could read a newspaper through them, and he'd sell you the newspaper, too. The news butcher who had the run from Amarillo to Kansas City said that he'd worked with Red Skelton when Skelton was a news butcher on that run. Every time we saw him he told us again, because that was his only claim to fame and he had a bad memory.

I was a dedicated reader, but for those who weren't, the two days of inactivity were a time of boredom and restlessness, and the only semblance of action was bending an elbow in the club car. The railroads had bought a lot of new equipment after the war, and they tried to give good service to keep all their business from trickling away to the airlines. They had even hired hostesses to help mothers with their kids and tell people about places of historic interest along the way and assist the dumbheads who couldn't read timetables and smile a lot and utter pleasant innocuous remarks to make everybody feel good so they'd ride the train again.

We had no need of those services; our only contact with the hostesses was to smile in return and say that everything was okay and to try to put the make on them—but never with any luck. On the second night of one of our trips east, as the train tore along through central Kansas, Vic and Jim and Jack Blue and I were in the club car telling tales and keeping the breweries in business. Something that Jim had had to eat or drink didn't agree with him: he was breathing heavily and looked green around the gills. You have to give him credit, though; he hung right in there and kept on drinking. But after another beer the liquid seemed to be running out of the pores on his face as fast as he poured it down his throat, and his color had changed from green to red to white. Vic asked him if he needed a transfusion, and Jack said that he looked like death warmed-over.

Jim admitted to feeling a mite queasy, and said he thought he'd better get to the can just in case that churning in his guts wasn't a false alarm. The nearest men's room was in the adjacent car, the train was doing at least eighty on a rough roadbed, and that club car was jumping and rolling like a cooch girl with the St. Vitus dance. Jim shimmied his way down the car, and as he got to the door he met a hostess going the other way. All that wild motion got to Jim, and just as the hostess opened the door and smiled at him, he heaved his guts out all over that poor girl in her pretty uniform. Fortunately he didn't get any on her smile, but she was pretty well covered between the neck and the knees, giving you a good idea of what Jim had been eating. Jim couldn't take the time to apologize, because getting to the can was still his aim in life.

We were much surprised, because Jim was the best there was when it came to holding his liquor. Jack said you can't win 'em all, and Vic said it was lucky for us we didn't know that guy. There was considerable consternation and anger being manifested in the club car, someone went to get the conductor, and we decided to discreetly return to our seats. On the way, we checked the can to see if Jim was okay. He was down on his knees, leaning over the bowl, shivering and shaking like a dog shitting razor blades—but it looked like he'd live.

The very next trip back on the train we had the bad luck to encounter the same train crew. The conductor recognized us; he gave us the evil eye but didn't say anything. We had a fifth of bourbon, so we did our drinking in the men's room and stayed out of the club car. The first night out, Vic got friendly with a woman who, like a lot of travelers, had left her inhibitions at the depot. By the second night she was hot to trot, but when you're riding the day coach there simply isn't anyplace to consummate a great love affair. The plutocrats in the Pullmans had it made, but, as usual, the hoi polloi got the short end of the stick.

Vic and the woman had their minds made up, and the only way to stop them would have been to wreck the train. They waited until one o'clock in the morning, an hour after the club car had closed, with everybody asleep and no more traffic between the cars. So that's where they went, on the platform between the cars: dark and noisy, snow blowing through the cracks, and colder than a gravedigger's ass in the Klondike. Vic backed her up against the cold steel wall, they both dropped their pants down around their ankles, and went at it as best the conditions would allow.

At that moment along came the conductor, making his last tour of the train before ending his stint at Kansas City. He caught Vic and the woman *in flagrante delicto,* and was shocked beyond measure because it was the most flagrant thing he'd ever seen in forty-two years of railroading, and believe you me railroading wasn't all peaches and featherbedding and he didn't know what the world was coming to, and Vic said it wouldn't come to anything if dirty old men in uniforms didn't quit playing buttinski. Vic said later that the conductor was so surprised that he didn't know whether to shit or go blind or close one eye and fart, but he *was* the conductor which was the same as captain of a ship and this was obviously not a union made in heaven and his duty was clear, so he sternly stood there while Vic and the woman hauled up their pants and went their separate ways, under threat of being flung off the train into the next snowdrift if they even so much as looked cross-eyed at each other.

Vic was all for laying over a night in Chicago with this woman and doing things properly, but the next morning she wouldn't speak to him. The closer the train got to Chicago the more she realized that her inhibitions would be waiting for her on the station platform.

Not long after that the Old Man began sending us back on The Challenger on the Union Pacific, and we got to see a different piece of country. The train rides became less frequent, however, since the Old Man wised up to sending us east by car to save money. Of course that increased the wear and tear on us, and often the eastbound trip was more of a grind than coming out with a convoy. In 1950 we went back several times in the Old Man's 1942 Hudson, a car that was small and cramped and handled like a battleship. The Old Man liked to mention that because of his connections his car was the last one off the Hudson assembly line on December 31, 1941, when the government stopped all civilian auto production for the duration.

For a while, the Old Man used rental cars to get us east; we'd drop the cars in Chicago and ride the train to Detroit. Even that was too much expense to the Old Man's way of thinking. As soon as he bought his 1951 Hudson Super Six with overdrive we started driving that back, and towing it out on the convoy. After six or seven trips like that the Old Man could see that his Super Six would be a worn-out pile of rust in two years. But then he had a brainstorm, and put an ad in the transportation column of the *Los Angeles Times.* It read: "Responsible businessman will drive your car to eastern point, and pay all gas and oil." And that did the trick. Thereafter we had someone's private car for the eastbound trek. Except for those infrequent occasions when the Old Man had no business at all, that ad was in the paper for seven years straight.

The Old Man always ran true to form. When he began sending us back to Detroit by car he would pack as many bodies and as much equipment into the car as it would hold, as if a car were merely a huge steamer trunk, and the challenge was to see how much bulk could be stowed in the available space. When business was good this meant six men in the car, the trunk full of towbars, and suitcases stacked in a luggage carrier on the roof.

The Old Man usually was a couple of jumps ahead of us. When some aspect of the job was given a new twist, it was generally for the worse—for us. After ten trips east with five or six men in the car, we finally got our heads together and decided to complain; and if that didn't work, we'd resist. Part of our difficulty was that it was never the same collection of men—the turnover was too fast. When we did complain, it was no more of a problem than doubling-up in the hotel beds had been. The Old Man gave me thirty seconds of flinty-eyed stare, and then admitted that I had a legitimate point. We established an understanding: no more than four men in a car. The Old Man's word was good, and he stuck to the agreement. If he had five men to send back, he'd come up with two cars or one car and one railroad ticket.

Most of the cars were ordinary sedans, whose owners didn't care for the strain of driving across the country. But every now and again we got hold of something that gave us a glimpse of how the other one half of one percent lived. The best car we ever had was a 1951 Jaguar Mark VI sedan that came our way in the spring of 1952. We had to take the bus to Palm Springs to pick up the car, which belonged to a wealthy middle-aged matron who disliked driving it because it didn't have an automatic transmission. She gave me the keys and a piece of scrap paper with a Flint, Michigan address, and said she didn't care what day I got there but to deliver the car before noon because she was usually out after that but not before ten because she wouldn't be up.

I was constantly amazed by the manner in which people turned over their cars to us. There were two basic patterns, both of them extremes, neither of them related to a car's caliber or to the wealth of its owner. Half the population will not let you near their cars unless you sign your life away, and the other half will hand over the keys as casually as doling out a stick of chewing gum.

There were four of us in the Jaguar: Mickey and I, a kid nicknamed Fat who was just out of the army, and a motorcycle rider from Dayton, Ohio named Floyd Aarons. But it's not Jewish, Floyd said, even though it sounds that way. Floyd had one of those old Scotch-Irish faces, like the hillbillies who had arrived in the Appalachians in the late eighteenth century and had been there ever since, inbreeding. Floyd admitted that his folks were from the hills, but he himself was no ridgerunner and he had traveled around a lot and owned a big Indian cycle and wasn't just a hick from back in some holler. It was true that Floyd had been all over hell's half acre. He had the going fever, and he was always going somewhere or coming back. He made four or five trips for the Old Man, but that wasn't movement enough, and he was getting restless again.

Floyd told us about the time he was knocking around in Alaska. He was in Fairbanks in early January, when it was colder than a witch's tit and blacker than a whore's heart, and there wasn't much to do in Alaska at any time except fish and fuck, and in winter there isn't any fishing. Floyd picked up an Eskimo girl in a bar, just to change his luck, and took her up to his hotel room. She was willing but not wildly enthusiastic, and she was so unhelpful that getting her undressed was like trying to peel a one hundred and fifty pound banana one-handed.

While Floyd was working up a sweat, the girl discovered one of his Christmas presents sitting on the bedside table. It was a homemade cake, baked by Floyd's mother in Dayton. It had arrived just that day after six weeks in the mails, and was stale and dry and battered, and reduced to crumbs and rock-hard chunks. Floyd thought it inedible and was going to throw it out, but his klootch thought it first-rate fare. Floyd finally got her clothes off, and was working her over to see if he couldn't arouse a spark of passion, but she just lay on her back with her legs spread and ate that cake as fast as she could.

Floyd managed to get what he was after, and she got what she was after, too: Ma's cake, and she never even took notice of what Floyd was doing. Floyd confessed that he'd been pretty drunk, which helps take the sting out of a situation like that, but it sure is tough when you wake up in the morning and take a gander at what's been in bed with you. Floyd said the whole damned bed was full of cake crumbs, but what almost made him sick was to take a close look at that klootch in a good light. The only clean spots on her body were where he'd been licking her tits, and all things considered he figured he would have been better off if he'd fucked a knothole.

Talking about Alaska and other places he'd been made Floyd so travel-crazy that he couldn't stand the thought of going back and forth over the same piece of road for the Old Man. He apologized for quitting on short notice, but he just had to go someplace new. He got out of the car at the junction east of Kentland, Indiana, to hitchhike home to Dayton by way of Indianapolis. In Dayton he was going to switch his clothes around and then get on his Indian and get gone. We were sure sorry to see him go, because he was a good driver and a nice guy to have around, and whenever we thought about Floyd somebody would be bound to tell the story about the klootch who was queer for stale cake. An experience like that was enough to sour you on your mother's cake forever.

The Good Soldier

A good folly is worth what you pay for it.
Fables in Slang
George Ade

Fat's name was Alfred E. Thurston, but he had been called Fat ever since he was a kid in grade school. He wasn't so much fat as a bit overweight for his height, which was about five foot five. But you could see that a kid with his build was likely to run to fat later on. When he hit fifty, you could picture him with a big beerbelly hanging over his belt.

Fat always said that if he could work up the willpower to quit smoking he'd be able to do anything, but he could never quit smoking. Even if he had quit, that wouldn't have been the end of his problems. He would also have to quit guzzling beer and quit eating eggs and ham and potatoes and toast every morning for breakfast and chicken-fried steak and fried potatoes and bread and butter for dinner and pie twice a day, and he'd have to quit blowing his dough in on every split-tail he ran across. But that would only be the beginning. Once he had the don'ts whipped he'd have to start right in on the do's, which would be a damned sight harder. He would have to settle down and get up early in the morning and work hard and save his money and eat sensibly—and then don't smoke and drink and fuck around and all the rest of that, and not just for a while but for the rest of your life.

Well, that didn't seem like much of a future for a guy who was only twenty-two and had already acquired a good collection of bad habits, and was comfortable with them. Someone with no more willpower than Fat was better off drifting with the current and partaking of life as his habits moved him. Anything else would only make him unhappy. Everybody knew that those bad habits would kill you in the end, but they were what made life worth living.

Fat was from Ypsilanti. If you were raised in Ypsi and didn't finish high school, you didn't have much chance of ever seeing your name up in lights. When you dropped out of school you couldn't expect to get much of a job—maybe pumping gas or stock clerk at a market, and if you didn't starve before you came of age you could move up to driving a taxi or swamping on the freight docks.

Of course if your health was good and you had a combination of good and bad luck, you would be drafted. The army didn't look like such a good bet, because you were free, white, and twenty-one and didn't want somebody shoving you around for two years, but on the other hand it looked like a better deal than you could get staying in Ypsi where there weren't any opportunities and not much to do except get drunk on Saturday night and probably wind up in a fight at the Riverside Tavern. In the army you could learn a trade, and they'd house you and feed you and give you thirty days of paid vacation a year and maybe you could get overseas. You wouldn't have to worry about where your next meal was coming from, and all in all there might be enough benefits to make up for losing your freedom for a couple of years.

Fat dropped out of high school when he was halfway through his junior year, and he was sorry later but by then he wasn't about to go back to school with all those wet-behind-the-ears kids. He worked around for a couple of years, and sat on his butt and drew unemployment when he couldn't find a job. Then the army got him, but instead of teaching him a trade they issued him an M-1 and put him in a rifle company. Although he didn't learn anything that was of any use to anybody, he did get to spend most of his two years in Germany in the Army of Occupation, which in those days was a pretty good deal because your bucks would go a long way. You couldn't get a girl for a deck of Luckies or a candy bar any more, but you could sure get your ashes hauled for a few marks, and if you met the right girl and wanted to set up housekeeping off the base, there was nothing to stop you. Fat shopped around, and before long he fell madly in love with a good-looking fraulein who worked as a stenographer for the Military Government, and they got themselves a little flat a couple of miles from the base and settled down just like man and wife.

Fat had never had a steady girl before. He and his schatzi got along great for a few months, making out like minks every night and between them having enough money to do anything they wanted. It was true what they said about those European women—they sure knew how to treat a man. Fat's schatzi treated him like a king and didn't give him any lip, and they lived higher off the hog than Fat had ever been able to do in Ypsi. Fat said he made only one mistake, and that was that he spoiled her rotten and it went to her head. One day they got into a big argument because she didn't keep the place as clean as Fat thought she should, so Fat told her to shape up or ship out, and she talked back to him for the first time, and Fat belted her one right in the chops and knocked her ass-over-teakettle down the stairs, and her face got busted all to hell and gone.

That was the end of Fat's only love affair, and it made him kinda blue when he thought about it because everything was perfect and would have stayed that way if that dumb kraut hadn't run off at the mouth. Fat had been thinking of reenlisting, and maybe even going for twenty so he could retire on half pay at the age of thirty-nine, but when he busted up with his schatzi he lost his enthusiasm for the army. When his two years were up he drifted back into civilian life with the same mixed feelings about the army that he'd had before he was drafted. He had some good times in the army, and he did most of his hitch in Germany and lived the good life with his schatzi. On the other hand, he'd been a nice clean-cut kid when he went into the army, but when he got out he was cynical and a hard drinker. That good German beer had messed him up, and the blowup with his schatzi had cooled him on the course of true love. He had become a pretty fair boozer, and he believed in getting his tail where he could find it and screw that settling down.

Fat may not have learned a trade in the army, but he did learn how to soldier and he took a lot of pride in it. His company had a weekly competition to see who could present the most soldierly appearance, with shoes and belt buckle gleaming, razor-sharp crease in the pants, spotless rifle, close shave and haircut, bunk made up so tight you could bounce a quarter on it, and all your gear laid out just so. At the high-water mark of his military career, Fat could soldier well enough to win two weeks out of three, which earned him some extra time off and put him in the good graces of officers and NCOs. Fat had the notion that being a good soldier was the same as being a man, but when he got out of the army he realized that nobody in civilian life gave a hoot for soldiering, and if you tried to pull that spit-and-polish crap they'd laugh you right out of town.

Fat had to think it through again, and like most everyone else he couldn't come up with any good answers. There were various schools of thought, but most of them were crude and shallow, and they didn't apply in all situations. How many guys you had hit in the mouth had validity to it, but it was only good for local, short-term satisfaction, and couldn't be used as a credential. How many women you had seduced and what a cocksman you were was somewhat better and more permanent, because most men were playing that game and if you played it better than they did there was just a chance they would look up to you.

Driving on the highway was to be more of a man than those who went to work at the same place every morning and came home in the afternoon without having been anywhere, and without having done anything you could put your finger on—just putting nuts on bolts or shuffling papers or dealing in abstractions that vanished the instant you stopped thinking about them. Driving over the road gave you power: it made you a bigger man than the guy who putted around in the family sedan, and it gave you freedom—or the illusion of freedom, which is just as good—even though all you were doing was working for wages. When the sun warms your face and the wind ruffles your hair and you're headed on down the road toward the horizon, then you're living free and easy the way a man should, and you're doing a man's work.

The nature of the job guaranteed that everyone on it would think about the short term—the long run would have to take care of itself. You could consider only one trip at a time. Arriving in Los Angeles and delivering the cars or trucks was so final that it was not possible to regard the future as anything other than an emptiness having no connection with the present.

Each trip was complete in itself, with proper beginning and end, and constituted a measurable achievement. We never stopped to think about where the job was leading or what we might be doing in a year or ten years. You have to do something to fill up the time, and constant motion, for those of a certain temperament, is the most satisfactory way. We lived our lives on the surface, and left the depths alone. The Old Man, too, led such a life. He operated his modest business as a means of filling the empty days. We were his agents in this enterprise, and he was ours.

When Fat came on the job he could talk of nothing but the army, and of his schatzi whom he had loved and lost. We kidded him a lot, saying that he'd found a home in the army but that he hadn't been smart enough to know it. Civilian life was cold and cruel, and you had to hustle to make a living. No more free room and board and travel and paid vacations—nothing but long hours and bad pay, with no chance for advancement and no prospect but growing old and dying. Whereas if he'd stayed in the army and kept his nose clean and knew how to soldier, maybe in a half a lifetime he would get to be top sergeant, and could spend his declining years drinking coffee and shoving people around. But Fat said that the army was too chickenshit to suit him, and he didn't mind working hard so long as the boss wasn't forever looking over his shoulder. And besides, if he'd re-upped they probably would have sent him over to Korea to get his ass shot off.

Fat's home was in Willow Run Village, a complex of "temporary" wartime structures built to house workers at the Ford bomber plant at Willow Run, just outside Ypsilanti. Like many other temporary wartime buildings, they would be used until they fell to the ground from their own weight. They had been constructed in the utilitarian barracks style of the war, and ten years later were plagued by peeling paint, broken windows, leaking roofs, crumbling foundations—a general decrepitude and disintegration that also characterized the inhabitants.

Most of the barracks dwellers were doomed to stay in Willow Run Village and go downhill with their dwellings. Either they had no other place to go or, if they knew of a better hole, lacked the means to get there. Many were unemployed, many were on welfare. Fat's old man was a lush, who came home only when he was in a bitter mood and wanted to beat on his wife and children and get his hands on the welfare money. When Fat got big enough to fight back, he and his old man had a knock-down drag-out battle that ended in a draw. But in a way Fat won, because his old man quit coming around. Fat became the breadwinner by default, which was more than he had bargained for, and he was relieved when the army took him away from all that.

When he was discharged he naturally returned to Willow Run Village, the only home he had. He got a job hacking for the Veterans Cab Company, but right from the beginning he was in over his head. His mother and younger sister expected him to bring home the bucks, and Fat was so tied down that he hardly had time to do any living. A month after he got back he knocked up a girl he'd known in school, and since she was strong for getting married Fat figured it was time to leave town. So he went to Detroit and got on one of the Old Man's convoys, because he'd never been to California and wanted to see the country before he put on a ball and chain. Fat claimed that he wasn't responsible for knocking up the girl anyway. Even though she had only been fucked twice in her life, it was by the army and the navy.

All the buildings in Willow Run Village were one-story, with two dwelling units in each building. There were grassy areas at the sides and in back, but it wasn't like in the suburbs. Nobody took care of the grass, and it had all grown over in weeds. The terrain was flat, there was a lot of open space, and there were trees close by in several directions, but the instant you entered one of those dwellings you felt as though you were in a tenement: stuffy, badly lit, odors of inedible cooking, the sound of raucous music coming through the wallboard, some damned baby bawling its lungs out. It was enough to give you claustrophobia or the screaming meemies, and you could see right away why Fat wanted to bug out of there. It was homes like that that made a man go traveling.

O Beautiful, for Spacious Skies

> In the United States there is more space
> where nobody is than where anybody is.
> This is what makes America what it is.
>
> ***The Geographical History of America***
> **Gertrude Stein**

During late 1950 and most of 1951 the Old Man's business was scarce and spotty. Twice there were flurries of taxis. The Old Man got himself out of mothballs and came back on the road, and by running two crews we finished off the taxis in a couple of months. Then there was merely a trickle of Divcos to sustain us.

A guy who started driving about the same time as Fat was Glenn Miles, another nice clean-cut kid who was 4F because of bad eyesight so he didn't get all messed up by the army. But in addition to that, Glenn had a lot of other advantages over Fat. Glenn came from a stable home in Pontiac, his father had worked twenty years at the Pontiac factory, and was even loyal to the breed. He never owned anything but a Pontiac, and swore up and down that they were the best cars made.

Glenn's father might drink a beer at home on a Saturday afternoon, but he never went near the taverns. He was a first-rate example of an honest, reliable, sober, industrious workingman of the type that was going out of style because all the young guys had got used to enjoying the easy money you could make after the war and they figured the world owed them a living because they didn't know what the Depression was like, but Glenn had been raised right and was going to turn out as good a man as his father only he would probably go into business for himself instead of working at Pontiac where they treated you okay but there was nothing like being your own boss and getting ahead in the world. There was a world of opportunity for anyone who wasn't afraid of a little hard work, and don't pay any attention to those bums who badmouthed the United States which was still the greatest country on earth no matter what anybody said.

Glenn was no dummy, and of course he wouldn't believe a line of baloney like that if you paid him. But though he and the rest of us scoffed at all that old hogwash that they'd been filling us full of ever since we were in diapers, secretly everyone knew that it was the Lord's truth. You got it in your mother's milk and breathed it in the air and sopped it up from your history lessons in school, and it was in your bones whether you knew it or not. Each man translated it into his own terms, and made it work to suit his purpose. If you wanted to roll down the road, that was okay—The U.S. of A. was a great place to live in and see. If you wanted to work a steady job and save your money, that was okay—it's the only way to amount to something. If you wanted to work just enough to keep your head above water, that was okay—it's a free country. If you wanted to start your own business and work long hours so as to be independent and not owing nobody for nothing, that was more than okay—that's what made America what it is today. If you had git up and git, the sky was the limit—because this was the greatest place on earth just as sure as God made little green apples.

That's what everybody thought at the outset, but after they'd been around for a spell and had some of the stuffing knocked out of them, they knew that they couldn't make the grade by working for wages.

Glenn's awakening was yet to come. Driving cross-country was an extended vacation for him. He was riding the crest of the wave, and had no fear that he would ever take a fall. It was just a lark—an interlude of irresponsibility before he buckled down to serious living. Glenn had some experience installing furnaces, and figured to start his own business. He wasn't afraid of hard work, and because he was honest and would do top-notch work and stand behind it, he knew that he'd be able to meet the competition. If you had the know-how and applied a lot of elbow grease, you couldn't miss.

Glenn had an even temperament and a good sense of humor, and everybody liked him—except when he talked about going into the furnace-installing business. Then Ben said that Glenn had shit for brains, and Freeman Morse said that he didn't know his mule from an oasis. Fat halfway wanted to stick up for Glenn, because he sometimes wistfully thought that he too would like to be in business for himself—maybe take a lease on a service station. If he pumped enough gas and lubed enough cars and stayed off beer for a while, maybe he could scrape up enough for the down payment on a tandem-axle Ford or Jimmy, and hire himself and his rig out on construction jobs. Or maybe a cabover Dodge and get into the haulaway business. And then he could buy a second tractor and a third, and hire some good men to drive them—and if you kept right at it you could build up a thriving business and before long you'd have to take your money to the bank in a wheelbarrow. But of course Fat didn't say any of that when Ben and Freeman were around because he would have let himself in for scorn and ridicule. Ben and Freeman knew where it was at, and weren't bashful about saying so. If you put your nose to the grindstone and your shoulder to the wheel, you didn't have a Chinaman's chance of getting anything out of it except a raw nose and a flat shoulder.

The greatest threat to Glenn's plans for a prosperous future was his failure to recognize that life is just one damned thing after another. He figured that he had a handle on life because he'd got it all lined out ahead of time, and what could go wrong? He couldn't be convinced that to be on the road was the same thing as throwing your life up for grabs. There was no certainty, no solid ground, no way to make the future come true. You had cut yourself loose from the normal stream of events, the routine of school, job, home, and family. If you wanted to see the country and take your chances, you were on the right road. But if you were looking for the Main Chance, you'd made a wrong turn.

From eastern Kansas to Santa Fe our route followed the old Santa Fe Trail. It was slightly uphill all the way from the Missouri River to Trinidad, Colorado, and more often than not there was a headwind. Or there was a sidewind, which was just as bad. One day the wind would blow half of Oklahoma north to Nebraska, and the next day it would blow it back south again, bringing part of the Dakotas with it. Trying to keep a pair of stand-up Divcos between the fences in a strong sidewind was enough to drive a man around the bend. You were overloaded, underpowered, the wheels wobbled, and you could swear that you were steering with a rubber band. A ten-hour day grinding across Kansas gave you aching arms and shoulders, and a stiff right leg from holding the gas pedal on the floorboard all day. The only respite from the constant struggle was going through the occasional town, where the houses and trees blocked the wind and you could back off the gas a bit to cut your maximum speed of thirty-five down to the legal limit.

If we were on schedule we stayed the third night of the trip in Ottawa, Kansas. The hotel was an old frame building a block off the main drag, next to Monkey Wards. Like all the small-town hotels built forty and fifty years earlier, it was three-quarters empty at any given time, having lost its trade to the new motels on the outskirts of town. Ottawa was a sedate town, offering nothing more exciting than a roller-skating rink—no way for the drivers to get into trouble. After a couple of watery beers and a big chicken-fried steak at Cusick's Café, we hit the sack early.

On the fourth day we went out across long rolling hills, much to the surprise of the new drivers who had always thought that Kansas was dead flat. We passed Agricola (Fat was mighty smug because he knew that the word meant "farmer" in Latin, and of course he felt the impress of cultural superiority) and Williamsburg, a nice little town that was going downhill fast because it was too close to Ottawa and Kansas City, and the young people left town as soon as they finished high school.

We did the fifty-five miles to Emporia in one jump, filled up with cut-rate gas at Voight's, then did another forty-five miles to Florence where we'd be just in time for fruit pies hot out of the oven at the Home Café. Florence and many other towns still had brick streets in the early fifties, but they were soon covered over with blacktop. Then they built a bypass at Florence, and we didn't go through town any more. Instead of hot home-baked pie we got cold pie at the truck stop that had its pies produced in a factory somewhere.

After Florence came Peabody and Newton and then Hutchinson, which had huge grain elevators, oil and gas wells, and salt mines. They were making money every whichway. We gassed up again at Voight's main station, and had lunch in a small diner—seven or eight stools at an L-shaped counter, and that was it. We and other drivers and wheat farmers were the only customers the diner ever had. It put out good solid fare for a bargain price, and was run by one of those weather-beaten plainswomen who must have been forty-five the day she was born. She was a pleasant old gal who kept a spick-and-span place. It was just like home, with your sweet-natured but no-nonsense maw dishing up solid grub and lots of it, as though she was concerned about your welfare and was looking out for you.

West of Hutchinson the country flattened out, there were fewer trees, and the towns were farther apart. We did another forty-five miles to Stafford where we stopped at Mom's Café for our afternoon coffee. There was a good-looking girl working behind the counter at Mom's. She was the corn-fed type, and had big tits that weren't too well controlled by a loose and low-cut uniform. Fat had learned what stool to sit on, and when the girl leaned forward to do the dishes in the sink, Fat would fasten his eyeballs on the view. That girl's uniform fit so loose that you could look down the front of it and see what color socks she was wearing.

About a year after Fat came on the job the spoilsport highway department relocated the road so that it cut through the edge of town rather than going down the main stem, and we never went to Mom's again. Sometimes on the way east by car Fat would argue in favor of going to Mom's—for pie, he said, but we all knew it was for the watermelons—but we always had the bit in our teeth and didn't want to take the time to go half a mile out of our way. Fat would be disgusted because we were so unobliging. Red told him that he was old enough to be weaned and he should put those childish desires behind him, and Ed Polacek said that those farm girls tended to age quick and by now her tits would be hanging down to her waist and the sight would turn his stomach. Fat said that he wasn't asking for the moon, but it was his ambition to put one of those beauties in his mouth and the other in his ear, and play telephone.

The next town that amounted to anything was Kinsley, which had a sign along the highway saying that it was the same distance from both New York and San Francisco. They seemed proud of that, as though it made them feel that they were at the center of things—or else mighty pleased to be far from both those places. West of Kinsley the trees disappeared, except for in towns and along streams. Between Kinsley and Dodge City there were three clusters of grain elevators that passed for towns. One of them was called Spearville, and Ed said he remembered that town from the movie *Dodge City* starring Errol Flynn, and Ben Kuhel wanted to know how come he remembered crap like that. Ed was teed off, and said it wasn't his fault what he remembered.

Dodge City was the end of the fourth day's run, and we put up at the Trail Inn Hotel, a clean, comfortable old firetrap that might have been where the cowboys stayed at the end of the cattle drive from Texas. Invariably there was a one-way driver who was excited about taking a gander at Boot Hill, but we'd straighten him out—tell him that it was a dummied-up tourist trap made to catch dummies like him, and the nearest thing to excitement he could find would be a glass of three-two beer. And then we all went to Jack's Café, which had the best pork chops in the state.

Dodge City was right smack on the hundredth meridian. West of there the rainfall was less than twenty inches a year. The grass grew short instead of long, and if you plowed the ground and didn't irrigate, it might all blow away.

From Dodge to La Junta, Colorado—210 miles—we followed the Arkansas River, a strip of green through a gray and tan country. The highway, the railroad, and the river ran on together, with towns strung along them at regular intervals—county seats about fifty miles apart, and smaller towns in between. At Cimarron was a big sign boasting about the Cimarron Crossing of the Santa Fe Trail, just six blocks off the highway, but we never went there. At Garden City was a sign saying that it was the home of the largest zoo in Kansas and the largest free municipal swimming pool in the world. People were sure proud of the damndest things—a big hole full of water.

West of Lakin the road climbed gradually up a succession of low swelling hills, and when you reached the last and highest one, just above the town of Kendall, you had a view to the southwest that was as good as you could have had from a mountaintop. You could see twenty or thirty miles across the brown and gray plains spotted with black cloud shadows. Although there was an occasional farmhouse or grain elevator, they seemed to be part of the natural landscape and not erected by men. You had the feeling that the country was uninhabited, had never been traversed, and perhaps was sterile and not capable of supporting life. If you can get high enough above the land, most of the country looks like that. The great American scene: empty, barren, and abstract.

We got gas and coffee in Syracuse, a nice green oasis in all that emptiness, and made it to La Junta for a late lunch and another load of gas at Buzz's Shamrock station. The afternoon was a long uphill grind into the sun—eighty miles to Trinidad, with no towns to speak of. Bloom was the largest place—about ten battered frame houses, most of them deserted. The country was sagebrush and dry arroyos, the kind of territory the Indians usually got stuck with. Way off to the right was Pikes Peak, and as we came closer to Trinidad we could see the Sangre de Cristo range. Ten miles out of La Junta, at the top of a rise, was a state historical marker, saying that this was the Santa Fe Trail and the route taken by Kearny's Army of the West in 1846, and that nearby you could still see the ruts made by the covered wagons. I suppose that if we'd climbed the fence we could have seen the ruts, but no one ever did that.

Every now and again someone would be carrying a Brownie, and he'd take a snapshot of the sign.

We stopped at the general store at Thatcher, and if the weather was nice we stood outside, drinking soda pop and listening to the wind blow. Maybe the guy with the Brownie would take some shots of the other drivers standing in front of the Divcos.

Trinidad was a poverty-struck burg in the foothills. It had started as a coal-mining town, but the mines had folded and there were a lot of unemployed Mexicans standing around. The business section had narrow streets and old, rundown stone and brick buildings, and on the edges of town were unpainted shacks and crumbling adobes.

The last stretch of the day was the slowest one—crawling up Raton Pass at ten to fifteen miles an hour, and crawling down the other side in third gear so that the Divcos wouldn't run away with us. The state line was right at the pass, and before the New Mexico Port of Entry moved up there we sometimes stopped anyway for the view and to let the picture-takers do their stuff.

In Raton we stayed at the Palace Hotel, a second floor walk-up across from the depot. We'd get up early the next morning even though we were only going to Las Vegas—108 miles—to lay over. The road runs due south along the edge of the High Plains, with the Sangre de Cristo range—the southern end of the Rockies—a few miles to the west. We did forty miles to Springer where we gassed up at Al Jenne's Skelly station on the curve going out the south end of town, until in 1952 they relocated the highway and left Al sitting out there with a gas business on the road to nowhere.

A few miles south of Springer we'd get our first glimpse of Wagon Mound. Up close, Wagon Mound was just a big rocky hill, but from a distance—coming at it from the north—it looked like two yoke of oxen hauling a covered wagon. From twenty miles away you could see only the upper parts, and the oxen looked as though they were rising out of the ground—like a prophecy of the migration to come.

We didn't stop in Wagon Mound, nor anywhere else on that stretch of road. You couldn't get so much as a decent cup of coffee between Springer and Las Vegas. Wagon Mound had a roadside ptomaine stand. And Watrous, twenty miles farther on, had only a garage and a bar and a general store, and was slowly falling back into the dust. There was something peculiar about food and drink in the whole state of New

Mexico. They hadn't figured out how to make a decent hamburger, the coffee was so weak you could see the bottom of the cup, and the chili was hotter than the hinges of hell. One spoonful made you sweat like a man trying to shove soft butter up a wildcat's ass with a red-hot poker.

We made Las Vegas by midmorning, checked into the hotel, and settled down for our day of rest. We stayed at the Castaneda Hotel, next to the depot. It had once served the railroad passengers, and still had a semblance of its former class. The lobby furniture was made of heavy dark wood, upholstered in black leather studded with big brass buttons. The beds were brass, and the rooms had matching dressers and bedside tables and rocking chairs, and there were white enameled pitchers on the tables. The hotel was built in 1897, and in 1899 Teddy Roosevelt and his Rough Riders held their first annual reunion there.

When we had a lot of business and the Old Man himself was on the road, the Castaneda Hotel was the only overnight stop he liked. On a warm summer evening, after he'd had his dinner, the Old Man would take a chair out to the long side porch, lean back on the hind legs, prop his feet on the railing, and puff away on a Corona Corona.

Now the Old Man was no slouch, and he carried himself and dressed so as to command his share of respect. Of course we always called him "Mister" to his face, and when he had his pockets on and his feet up and a fourbit cigar in his mouth, you could have sworn he was the Lord of the Manor. When you came up to him sitting on that porch you felt as though you ought to remove your cap and give a tug on your forelock.

The Loves of Our Lives

Woman would be more charming if one could fall into her arms without falling into her hands.

Epigrams

Ambrose Bierce

When we laid over in Las Vegas I always gave a double ration of money to those drivers who were on the draw—which usually was everybody. That way they could afford something to read and a few beers and a movie. What most of us did was to hire a cab and go to Joe's Ringside, a roadhouse just outside the city limits on the highway to Santa Fe. We'd have several drinks and a big steak dinner, and if it was a Friday or Saturday night we'd sit around for a spell after dinner and listen to the western band twanging and banging. About six months after we started going there, Joe brought in some strippers—and from then on the place was packed every night.

Las Vegas was a crumby little town, struggling along under the burdens of race hatred and corrupt local politics—which is par for the course in New Mexico. It was also the town where more of the drivers got into a jam than in any other town on the route. Not because it was a worse town than many others, but because we stayed there often enough to get to know it—and we had time on our hands. If we had laid over in a town such as Quincy, why inside of a year the Old Man's business would have been shot to pieces—all the drivers dead and gone, the victims of cirrhosis, busted heads, and exotic diseases.

Glenn Miles, who turned out to be more susceptible and contrary than anyone had suspected, got hooked up with the wrong woman in Las Vegas—or perhaps it was the right woman—and though we all did our dead level best to dissuade him from his folly, he persisted. He either screwed himself royally or lived happily ever after. We never found out which.

The love of his life was a waitress at Joe's named Flora. She was Mexican-American, had been married and divorced, and had a two-year-old kid. Glenn fell in love with Flora while she was serving him booze and steaks, and we always suspected that he got his liking for her confused with his liking for food and drink, which wouldn't make him the first man who had that problem. Glenn would see Flora every other week when we laid over with the Divcos, and sometimes he'd get a chance to see her or talk to her on the phone for a few minutes when we were eastbound by car. You wouldn't think that a romance could get off the ground under such conditions, but they only worked at it the harder to compensate for the lack of opportunity. Just five or six trips after Glenn first spoke to Flora and she smiled back, they had it all planned. Flora was going to pack up her kid and all her gear, and Glenn was going to transport the whole outfit back to Pontiac, where he would set himself up in the furnace-installing business.

We told him he'd better install himself some brains first, because Flora was taking him over the jumps and he didn't have the sense to see it. It looked to us as if Flora would do almost anything to get out of Las Vegas, which probably was true but possibly irrelevant. Once you subtracted our basic cynicism from the equation, what remained might have been entirely on the up and up. Glenn though it was real, and perhaps Flora did too.

One night when we were in town Flora got off work early, and came down to the hotel to see Glenn. They were up in Glenn's room, talking over their plans. About midnight Ben Kuhel came in from an evening on a barstool, full of beer and wanting to talk to someone. He saw the light under Glenn's door, and went right in without knocking. There were Glenn and Flora lying on the bed—*fully dressed!* Talk about peculiar behavior, that took the cake.

Ben wanted to know what in Christ's name they were doing with their clothes on, and how come he didn't fuck her? Glenn said that they were talking, which was the least plausible explanation he could have offered. Ben didn't believe a word of it, and advised Glenn to insist that she put out before he went to all the trouble of hauling her ass clear back to Michigan. He pounded on Freeman's door and woke him up and said he should come running if he wanted to see something funny. Freeman came running down the hall in his shorts, and laughed like crazy when he saw Glenn and Flora lying on the bed with their clothes on. He sat down in their rocking chair and tried to persuade them to get undressed. Glenn's only ploy was to try to persuade Freeman and Ben to leave. Glenn was mild-mannered and not very big, and even if he had wanted to use force he probably couldn't have fought his way out of a ditch full of cornflakes. An appeal to Freeman's and Ben's better judgment wasn't having any success, because they didn't have judgment better than what they were already using.

Freeman and Ben were the best of friends, but they both were hardheaded and had frequent fallings out. Freeman was big and strong and had a hair-trigger temper. Ben was scrawny but wiry, and wasn't afraid of anybody. For a few minutes they both tried to talk Glenn and Flora into bed to do things properly, but then Freeman, just to be taking the contrary view, said that By God it was a free country and if they didn't want to fuck they didn't have to. Ben told Freeman he was a dumb shitkicking hillbilly, and Freeman smacked Ben in the mouth and knocked him down. Ben jumped up and clobbered Freeman alongside the head with the enameled pitcher, and Freeman fell across Glenn and Flora lying on the bed. Ben and Freeman thought that was the funniest thing yet, and they both started laughing like crazy. The desk clerk came upstairs and told them to cut out all the racket or he'd call the cops, and I came out of my room and said we were getting up at five o'clock, as usual, and why didn't everybody go to bed and sleep it off?

Ben had a cut lip and Freeman had a cut ear, but they were friends again. They went down the hall to their rooms, laughing like crazy because they didn't know what the world was coming to.

On the way east we dropped Glenn off in Las Vegas to pick up Flora and the kid. About six months later Glenn came by the mounting yard in Detroit, just to say hello and to bullshit about old times. We had a few Divcos and a whole slew of taxis, so we were working steady and eating good and didn't have a worry in the world. We asked Glenn how he was making out, secretly expecting to hear that he'd busted up with Flora. He said that they were getting along just fine. He had rented a house, had a good-paying job at the Pontiac factory, his parents liked Flora and the kid, and he and Flora were expecting a kid of their own. He was saving his money and had his eye on a vacant building, and was just about ready to go into the furnace-installing business.

We tried to talk him into taking two weeks off and making a trip to the Coast with us just for old times' sake, but he said he couldn't do it. We went over to the Keeweenaw Bar to have a beer, but Glenn had coffee—said he didn't like to go home with beer on his breath. He was sure married, and we were sure surprised to see it. Most of those who drove for the Old Man had been married and unmarried—separated or divorced or just forgetting to go home, and some of them were crossing all those state lines to avoid alimony payments and the rest of that trouble. We wished Glenn good luck and he said the same to us. He said he'd come around again sometime, but he never did.

Al Rushton was on the job for about a year during the early fifties, and he too got hooked up with a woman in Las Vegas. Al was a good-looking guy with a slick tongue, and was able to talk himself into the affections of almost any woman he met—but he lacked staying power. He was from Springfield, Illinois, which was where he'd been born and raised and had to stay away from because he had been married and divorced there and wasn't making the alimony payments and his ex-wife had a warrant out for him. He had married a second time—another Springfield girl—but she tried to run his life and he walked out on her. The first wife and the second wife became acquainted, and now they were good friends and just itching to sink their claws into Al. So naturally Al felt a bit paranoid when we were in Illinois, but in any other state he kept right on with his winning ways. Al didn't believe in settling for just any old run-of-the-mill girl. He always aimed at the top of the line, being willing to lower his sights later on if the top was unattainable. Al always said he believed in traveling First Cabin.

What seemed to be the top of the line in Las Vegas were the strippers at Joe's, so that's what Al aimed at. He made a play for a girl who had been working the small-town strip circuit for about a year, and he scored right off. She was from Amarillo, and had thought that anything would be preferable to slinging hash and going to seed in her own hometown, and taking off her clothes three times a night paid better wages than she could get doing anything else. But she'd had her fill of that old grind, and was on the lookout for something better—and Al looked like it. The normal trade in Joe's consisted of drunken cowboys, greasy-haired Mexicans, and callow college boys with no money. Alongside a crowd like that, Al appeared downright exotic. He bathed more than once a week, looked good and dressed neatly, spoke well and had a big smile, always seemed to have plenty of folding money, and traveled to distant places—Detroit, Chicago, L.A.

Al swept her off her feet and into bed, and she was the happiest girl in the world to be taken away from that grubby life by such a gallant and charming gentleman. Al took her out to L.A. and they installed themselves in a house trailer in Sierra Madre, just east of Pasadena. The honeymoon lasted two days, and then Al had to go Detroit to make a trip with Divcos. It took several trips before the girl realized that she'd bought a pig in a poke. Al was gone ten or twelve days out of every two weeks, and he had barely enough money for his own grub, smokes, and beer. In order to eat, she had to get a job carhopping at a drive-in. When Al did hit town, all he wanted was to drink a few beers and roll in the hay until it was time to head east again. That was no kind of life for a girl whose best years were hopefully still ahead of her, so she flew the coop.

We came to town in our milk wagons, delivered them to the distributor, and Al grabbed the bus to Sierra Madre to grab himself some of that home life. But the trailer was empty. She had cleared out with all her gear, and Al's gear as well. She didn't leave a farewell note, but on the table were a quarter and two pork chops. The chops had been there a week and had turned green. Al shrugged it off—easy come, easy go. There were no legal problems, and women were like streetcars—there would be another one along in a minute.

When Vic Szafranski was on the job he'd had a woman in Las Vegas. She clerked in the five and dime, and was a confirmed old maid at age forty. You could see why, because she had a face that only a mother could love. But Vic wasn't interested in looks—he just wanted a convenient lay to occupy his layover day. Vic was too smart to confuse his short-term pleasure with whatever was going to happen next year and the year after that. In order to keep the affair going he had to let the old maid think that they would eventually get married, but that was standard operating procedure. When Vic quit driving for the Old Man, he just quit—never told that woman that he wouldn't be coming back.

Vic picked her up in a bar one evening when several of us were having a few before dinner. We didn't see her again after that, because Vic didn't bring her out in public. He spent all his time at her place, eating and drinking and laying over. Usually he didn't get back to the hotel until morning, just about the time the rest of us were getting up. He would come along the sidewalk with his head down, walking close to the curb, weaving in and out of the parking meters, bleary and bedraggled, seeming to be on his last legs. He wouldn't be in shape to get any breakfast down, but he drank lots of black coffee. We could remember what his woman looked like from the one time we'd seen her, and we enjoyed kidding Vic about her—especially when he was feeling half sick from too much drink and no sleep—but Vic had an answer for everything. She was skinny as a rail (the closer the bone, the sweeter the meat), taller than he was (a long board for a good teeter), and when it came to that ugly mug of hers, why he just threw a flag over her face and fucked for Old Glory.

I always worried that Vic wouldn't be in shape to drive. He was running on the rear of the convoy as mechanic, and after we left Las Vegas he would gradually fall behind and eventually disappear from view. When he got to Rowe, about halfway to Santa Fe, he stopped at the general store and had a can of Coors. He'd catch up to us at Santa Fe, where we were having coffee, and assert that the Coors had made a new man out of him, and that he was good for the rest of the day—and he'd be right. The only way you could tell that Vic had had a hard night was that his face didn't have any color, and his eyes looked like two pissholes in the snow.

The Screwing You Get

So we beat on, boats against the current,
borne back ceaselessly into the past.
The Great Gatsby
F. Scott Fitzgerald

The first two trips I made for the Old Man, in May and June of 1949, started from the backyard of the abandoned house near the intersection of Michigan and Wyoming in northwest Detroit. The Divco factory was in Macomb Township, to the northeast, and when the job got rolling steady in September the Old Man arranged to pick up his Divcos at the Spink Releasing Service, at the corner of Mound Road and Outer Drive.

Henry Gerber, who had worked for the Old Man long enough to become expert at beating down the price, made a deal for the Old Man's drivers to stay at the Mount Royal Hotel on Woodward Avenue. We got in for two dollars a head, each man in a plain room with the bath down the hall. The Mount Royal was about four miles out the avenue from downtown, next door to a synagogue and across the street from an Episcopal church. About half of the residents of the hotel were retired pensioners, and many of the others were permanent residents but still working, like Sammy who ran a one-man interior decorating business out of the trunk of his car.

The west side of Woodward was all white. It was unusual even to see a black face on that side of the avenue. East of Woodward were white and black mixed, but the whites were getting out and the blacks were coming in. The houses on the streets off of Woodward were single-family dwellings or two-story duplexes, forty to fifty years old. You could see how it had once been a neighborhood of middle-class respectability, but now it was on the downgrade and picking up speed. Many of the houses had been broken up into small apartments and single sleeping rooms. Half the people in the blocks just west of the avenue were from Kentucky and West Virginia. They and their immediate predecessors had come to Detroit during the war to make the big money in the defense plants. When they got laid off they went down home for a spell, but they always returned. They were permanently worried—worried about money, about getting a place to stay, about finding a job, and worried about the niggers who didn't look like they would stay on their own side of the avenue, and if you gave them an inch they would take over the whole city.

But for the most part the white side of the avenue lived as always—as though blacks didn't exist. The Mount Royal Hotel never refused a black—no black ever stuck his head in the door. The same was true of the bars and restaurants up and down the avenue. No one had the idea of sitting-in to integrate a place. The blacks weren't bold enough, and the whites wouldn't have held still for it. It would have upset the natural order of things. There were many white people who darkly predicted that Detroit was ripe for another race riot, sounding as though they welcomed the event and implying that the next time around they would do a better job of it. Others, a minority, said that there wouldn't be a riot—so long as the niggers kept to themselves and didn't try to barge in where they weren't wanted. To hear white people talk, you wouldn't think that they had any hard feelings against blacks. They simply didn't want to see them any more.

From the Mount Royal we took a bus across Holbrook and out Mound Road to Spink's. Holbrook went through several blocks inhabited by blacks and past the Champion Bar, which Ed Polacek, who had lived in Detroit all his life, said belonged to Joe Louis. Then through Hamtramck, which had more Polacks than Warsaw, and past the Chevrolet Gear and Axle plants, where we were strongly reminded of the kind of work some guys had to do to make a living, and then we didn't mind so much sweating and freezing for the Old Man and his starvation wages. The drivers who had done some time on the production line said that rather than do that again they would prefer to spend their days shoveling shit against a stone wall.

The bus turned left where Holbrook ended at the Sunoco refinery. Everywhere you went in Detroit were smokestacks, and everything looked old and gray and tired. None of us cared the least for Detroit, and we never would have gone there if that wasn't where they made cars and trucks. Maybe to Ed and a few others Detroit looked like home, and home is home even if it is ugly and dirty, but to most of us Detroit looked like the ass end of creation.

Ed was born in Detroit in 1919, the youngest of four children. His parents had come over from the Old Country when they were young, and had worked hard and saved their money and brought up a fine family in the American way. They came from Bohemia, and Ed was always quick to explain that when he said they were Bohemians he meant from that place in Europe—they didn't have any connection with the bohemians who lived in Greenwich Village and places like that. They were respectable people, he said. Ed's old man was a journeyman machinist and had worked more than thirty years at Ford's in Highland Park. When he was sixty-five he retired, and ten months later he died of cancer.

None of the four children turned out to be half so industrious and thrifty as their parents. Ed's oldest sister, Alice, had been married and divorced twice—mainly she lived on alimony payments. The next sister, Kate, supported herself as a secretary at an insurance company, and lived alone and didn't much like it. She was picky and choosey when it came to men, because she wanted someone who made decent money and was a clean-liver and had some ambition and thought about higher things than just sex. Not that Kate had anything against sex, because these were modern times and you had to accept it and she was only human and enjoyed a bit of hanky-panky now and then, but a girl couldn't be too careful and she wanted sincerity and fidelity before she went all the way. Three times she got close to marriage, but the strain of it was too great and she started hitting the bottle. After work she would go straight to her apartment, pull the blinds, peel off her girdle, and go to work on the sauce. And when that man came knocking at her door she would feel mean and bitter and tell him that he was ruining her life and not to bother coming around again, thank you.

Ed's brother Chuck was cut out of the same material. He started out okay when he left home, working hard and saving his money. But after the war his marriage went on the rocks and he became a boozer. He was laid off from his job at Dodge Main, and when his unemployment ran out and he was evicted because he couldn't pay the rent, a sympathetic bar owner gave him a sleeping room above the bar and a few bucks walking-around money in exchange for swamping out the place—and of course Chuck sampled the stock while he was swamping. Chuck and Kate and Alice were good people and had a soft spot for Ed who was the baby of the family, and if Ed was down on his luck they would always feed him and put him up on the couch.

In the late thirties it looked as though Ed would be the first member of the family to finish high school, but one night he was carried away by emotion and knocked up his girlfriend Rosie. The first Ed knew of it was one day when he came home from school and found his ma all red-eyed from crying. Rosie's old lady was sitting in the best chair, looking like the wrath of God and saying that either Ed did the right thing by Rosie or she would see to it that he went to reform school where he probably belonged.

It was the spring of Ed's junior year, and if he could have held out for another fourteen months he would have had his diploma and it might have changed his whole life. But Rosie's old lady was a staunch Catholic, and she knew of only one solution. Ed wanted to say Wait—or Yes, but later. But there was no waiting and no later. It was Ed's first experience with the screwing you get for the screwing you got.

Ed got into a sweat because he could see his life coming to an end before it had fairly started. He grabbed a change of clothes and went over to stay with Chuck, who had a good job at the time and a place of his own and was engaged to get married himself. Chuck knew his way around, and was sympathetic to Ed's problems and wasn't backward about giving advice. He told Ed that he had sure made a big mistake by not keeping it in his pants, but that it didn't make sense to let Rosie and her old lady crap all over him. After all, it takes two to tango, and if Rosie couldn't keep her legs crossed the way a decent girl should then she didn't have any squawk coming when she got caught. Ed said he could go along with that, but he was sure in a jam what with everybody ganging up on him and he didn't know what to do. Chuck said the only thing to do was take a trip somewhere. It wouldn't hurt him to see the country, and by the time he got back it would have all blown over.

They checked the ads in the paper, and the next day Ed signed on with an outfit that was taking new Buick taxicabs on towbars to Los Angeles. The outfit was willing to take Ed even though he was only seventeen—nobody cared too much about the rules in those days. If the kid could drive and wanted to go to the Coast, well why the hell not? Ed's driving experience was limited to a few turns around town in his old man's Essex, but he talked it up good and they said he could go. Chuck was envious because here was this green-as-grass kid brother of his going out to L.A. to see the palm trees and orange groves and movie stars, and Chuck had always wanted to go there himself to maybe take a crack at some of those small-town girls who went out to Hollywood to get into pictures but didn't make the grade, and were so hardup they would drop their laundry for the first guy who asked them.

When Ed was set to go, Chuck said he hoped the experience had taught him a lesson. It was all right to screw around, which was only normal, but you shouldn't do it close to home because it would always backfire on you. If you wanted to get some tail, do it on the other side of town where they don't know who you are. Chuck said that was the best advice he knew—Don't fuck where you eat.

On that spring morning in 1937 Ed and about twenty-five other men assembled in a vacant lot where the taxis were lined up. There were only twenty hookups, but they made it a practice to take several extra drivers in case some of them didn't pan out. Ed started out as one of the drivers, and when they had gone only five miles out Michigan Avenue he made a too-sudden stop at a red light and jack-knifed his hookup. The cars weren't damaged, but the towbar was ruined and Ed was afraid they wouldn't let him go to the Coast and he'd have to crawl back and face the music. But they put on a spare towbar, installed one of the spare drivers, and told Ed to ride for a spell to see how it was done. Later on they let him drive again, and by the time they hit L.A. he was pretty handy at it.

Most of the drivers didn't have chauffeur's licenses. Over the years the pilot had collected several hundred dimestore photos of drivers, and the first night out of Detroit he shuffled through his collection and gave each man a picture that looked something like him. The next day the caravan stopped at the state police post at Kentland, Indiana, and every driver got a chauffeur's license. The pilot had a deal worked up with the state cops. The cops issued the licenses without looking hard at the pictures or asking any embarrassing questions, and the pilot gave the cops an extra four bits per head. When the caravan got to L.A. the drivers were allowed to keep the licenses and put their own photos on them, but they had to give back the other pictures for the pilot's collection.

They went down into southern Illinois, and crossed the Muddysloppy River at Cape Girardeau, Missouri, and then into Blytheville, Arkansas, where the whores were so thick that you to beat them off with a club. Twice while they were going through Arkansas, one of the drivers who lived down there pulled off on the shoulder, got out of his hookup, and walked off down a side road. Just a hillbilly who was headed back home and never had any intention of going to the Coast. But they had the extra drivers along, and if they ran short they picked up hitchhikers. Ed said that they even picked up three women hitchhikers, but not for driving. The pilot thought they might fuck their way to the coast, if they wanted a ride bad enough, but they weren't that hardup yet and got out at the next town.

Only the pilot and mechanic were drawing wages, and they also made a lot of money on the side—kickbacks from filling stations, cafes, and hotels. If you could promise to gas up twenty hookups or bring in twenty men to buy a meal, they were glad to give you a discount—times were hard all over. The one-way drivers got a dollar a day. They could eat well on that and still have something left. The pilot put them up two and three to a bed, and two nights they parked in truck stops and slept in their cars.

They crossed into Texas at Texarkana, and went clean across the state to El Paso. Way in the western part of the state, near Sierra Blanca, one of the drivers put his hookup in the ditch. The fenders and one grill were banged up some, but that was the only damage on the trip, which was better than average.

From El Paso they went to Las Cruces and Lordsburg and Tucson and Gila Bend and across the Colorado River at Yuma, and Ed was about floored when he got his first look at California and it turned out to be a desert. They went through a few miles of big sand dunes that looked just like the pictures of the Sahara Desert in his geography book at school, and at El Centro they turned right and went up the valley to Indio. And there in all that sand and the hot sun were a whole raft of tall palm trees growing dates, which flabbergasted Ed because it was like something out of the Arabian Nights, and if he hadn't seen it he wouldn't have believed it.

The pilot said that most of the year Indio was the last place on earth for a white man to be caught dead in, but in February they had a date harvest festival that made the Mardi Gras look like an old ladies' sewing bee. The festival lasted a week, and toward the end of the week everybody was so friendly that there was free beer and free ass for all comers, and the feasting, frolicking, and fucking went on until hell couldn't hold it. In fact, the main reason that Indio was such a deadass place most of the year was because they were getting over the last festival and getting wound up for the next one, and there wasn't much of anybody who lived there year around anyway except wetbacks and played-out whores who couldn't scrape up enough cash to get out of town. Ed filed that away, and thought that it would be great to hit Indio at festival time some year, and guzzle a lot of beer and get his rocks off for free.

At the time, though, he was glad to get away from a godforsaken place like Indio and out of that valley which they said was below sea level all the way from Indio to the Mexican border, and Ed thought they were pulling his leg. They went out past some roadside date stands and a billboard advertising something about the sex life of the date—which didn't make sense—and past Thousand Palms and up Whitewater Grade in a big headwind with sand flying through the air.

When they got up to Banning and Beaumont at San Gorgonio Pass the country looked greener and easier on the eyes, and when they went down the hill into Redlands and saw the palm trees and the flowers and all the plants that Ed didn't know what they were, he knew that at last he was in the real part of California and it was just the way he had expected. From Redlands clear through Ontario and Pomona there were orange groves on both sides of the road for as far as you could see, and because they were in good time the pilot stopped the caravan at a stand where they had all the orange juice you could drink for a nickel.

When they hit L.A., Ed got himself a room at the downtown YMCA on Hope Street, even though he didn't have any use for those Christers, but the rooms were cheap and they didn't push you about the religious crap. Ed had left Detroit with ten bucks that Chuck gave him, and he had been able to save two bits a day out of the buck the pilot gave him. So he was able to stay afloat for a few days until he found a job.

A seventeen-year-old kid had to take what he could get, and what he got was a job pearldiving in a greasyspoon café. He had to put in twelve hours a day, and when he had time off, if he wasn't all fagged out, he would go out to Hollywood to see if he could spot some movie stars, or down to Pershing Square to listen to the drunks and the Reds and the crazy old people and the Bible thumpers spouting off about sin and damnation and socialism, or out to MacArthur Park to horse around and maybe meet some girls but he never could make the grade, and twice he took the Red Car down to Long Beach to see the ocean and hit the amusement park where he had heard you could meet some pretty free and easy girls, but he was always shy of money and didn't score.

It was okay at first, but it wore thin in a hurry. Living at the Y was cheap, but Ed hadn't figured on washing the crap off of someone else's dishes. And besides, most of the guys at the Y were as queer as a three-dollar bill, and a clean-cut kid like Ed had to keep his back to the wall in the showers because you could never tell who wanted to play drop the soap.

A month of that was enough. Ed was getting dishpan hands from his job, keeping away from the fruits and the nuts was driving him goofy, and he was homesick so bad that he was dead certain that he wanted to marry Rosie and have the kid and get a good job and settle down and prove to everybody that he was okay. He knew that he could do it, too, because he wasn't just a fucking bum like most of the other guys who had come out on the caravan. He came from a respectable family, and his old man had worked at Ford's for thirty years.

Ed bundled up his clothes and hit the road for Barstow and Salt Lake, so as to see a different piece of country on his way home. Somewhere along the Lincoln Highway in Wyoming a rancher gave him a lift. The rancher took a liking to Ed and offered him a job. Ed took him up on it, and stayed on the ranch for six weeks. He did a lot of hard work just to earn his keep and a few bucks pocket money, but there was no place to spend money anyway, and after he got over his sore muscles he didn't mind the hard work. He felt good working out of doors, and thought he looked pretty rugged too, because he had one hell of a suntan on his face and hands. The rancher and the other hired hands treated him real good and wanted him to stay on, but he couldn't see it. There wasn't any chance for advancement, and Ed had the ambition to get ahead and be somebody. He didn't want to be like the other hands, who went to town once a month to fuck the whores and get sick drunk and blow all their dough. And besides, he had heard that in the wintertime in Wyoming it was cold enough to freeze the balls off a brass monkey, and the snow was asshole-deep to a big Red Indian. All in all, it was better if he went back to Detroit and did the right thing by Rosie. He was man enough to take his medicine, and anyway he wanted to marry Rosie and have a family and get a good job, and he could go to night school until he got his diploma.

And that's just the way it turned out. Ed and Rosie got married. Both families helped out with some money and enough furniture to get them started. Ed got a job pumping gas and greasing cars, and took a course at night school. Rosie had the kid, which was a girl and just as good-looking as Rosie. Everything was going along as smooth as a greased pig, and Ed figured that he had the world by the ass on a downhill drag. But when the kid was almost a year old she came down with meningitis, and in two weeks she died.

After that, nothing went right. Rosie sat around the apartment and cried all the time, and Ed started going out nights with a bunch of the guys and drinking a lot of beer. In two months Rosie picked up and went home to her old lady. Ed felt so lousy that he said to hell with everything, and he threw up his job and quit going to night school. He got kicked out of his apartment because he didn't pay the rent, so he went over to Chuck's place and lay around all day drinking Chuck's beer until Chuck's wife got disgusted and told Chuck either he goes or I go, so Ed was out in the cold again.

He could hardly believe what had happened. Here he was, only nineteen, and he had been all the way up and all the way back down. By age nineteen his life had already become just one damned thing after another. Getting married to Rosie was about the last deliberate, considered decision that Ed ever made. After that he let himself go, and blew around the country in front of the changing winds.

For a kid without a diploma and little experience, there wasn't much work to be had. He drifted from one pick-me-up job to another, and because he had lost his apartment he drifted from one couch to another —Kate's, Alice's, and Chuck's in turn, only a few days at a time in each place so that he wouldn't wear out his welcome. After a while he got into the CCC, and spent ten months at a camp in the national forest on the Upper Peninsula. It was hard work but a good clean life, and Ed thought that it was the best thing that could have happened to him. It straightened him out again. He stopped thinking about Rosie and the kid all the time, and of course he was off beer and didn't feel as though his life was on the skids. His only regret was that he hadn't stayed on that ranch in Wyoming.

In early 1941 he was back down in Detroit again, which was the only home he had even if it was no great shakes. In a weak moment he let himself get talked into going to work at Ford's. After four hours on the production line Ed figured that he wasn't cut out for that kind of work. When the lunch break was over and the strawboss hollered at him to get his ass in gear, Ed told him to go take a flying fuck, and he quit. He had a half a day's pay coming, but he was too proud to go back and get it.

Later in the year he was caught in the draft, and found himself getting free room and board and twenty-one dollars a day once a month. They made an ambulance driver out of him, and he spent a year in California driving between L.A. and Banning and the field station at Desert Center, hauling guys who had sunstroke or the clap or had shot themselves in the foot. In 1943 they shipped him to North Africa, and even though the fighting was almost over and he was nowhere near the front lines, it bothered him a lot just being there. He got so down in the dumps that he couldn't even crawl out of the sack in the morning.

First thing you know he was hauled to the hospital, where they said that he had a nervous breakdown and was about as useless as tits on a bull, so they shipped him back Stateside and gave him a medical discharge. When he went home to Detroit he could have cleaned up if he had taken a job in a shop and worked a lot of overtime, but he didn't think that was any kind of work for a self-respecting white man, and he didn't see why he should have to work with a bunch of niggers and hillbillies. The one thing he couldn't take was the boss forever looking over his shoulder, so he went hacking for Checker Cab where you could pretty much be your own boss and not have to take any guff. It was congenial work for Ed, and he stayed with it. Now and then he would have a run-in with the dispatcher and they would give him the gate, or he'd quit for a spell because business was slow and he figured he was better off drawing unemployment, but Checker would always take him back.

Ed never saved a nickel. The only money he had was whatever was still in his pocket from the last paycheck. Within a week after he quit or was canned, he was flat broke. If he hadn't had family in Detroit he would have had to hit the missions for a bowl of soup and a sermon, or else turn himself in to the Salvation Army.

In 1951 Ed was broke and out of a job. Because he was at loose ends he thought he'd go out to the Coast to see what he could scare up, so he signed on with one of the Old Man's convoys of Plymouth taxis going to L.A. He mentioned the trip he'd made in 1937 with the Buick taxis, and we realized that it had been an outfit run by one of the Old Man's pilots. It was as if nothing changed in those fourteen years. Ed was down on his luck, and because there was nothing to hold him he set sail for the golden shore. Los Angeles always looked good when you were in Detroit. It was far away and warm and exotic and maybe there was a chance to get out of the old rut and latch onto one of those good jobs that you'd heard so much about.

Ed happened to hit the Old Man's operation just at a time when there were lots of taxis and Divcos, and he became one of the regular drivers. He made even less money tow-barring than he had hacking, and he still couldn't save anything. But that cross-country travel beat most kinds of work. It was the nearest thing to real freedom that Ed had ever heard of, which was why the rest of us were doing it. Sometimes Ed would feel a bit nostalgic for that ranch in Wyoming, and when he was three-quarters stewed he would get to crying and moaning about Rosie, and the kid who had died. What really got to him was that Rosie had married a big wheel on the Detroit detective force, and she had three kids. He could never understand why a nice girl like Rosie had married a fucking cop.

Ed always hoped that he would meet a respectable woman, and they could get married and settle down, and he would quit the road for good and get a steady job. It was a vain hope. The only places Ed ever met women were bars and massage parlors. He blew his dough on beer and B-girls, and begrudged the few bucks that he occasionally had to shell out for clothes. He wouldn't buy a new pair of kicks until his soles were so thin that every time it clouded up his feet got wet. He didn't quite realize that he wasn't much of a bargain, because in his mind he was dead serious about quitting the road and settling down. But he never met any mind readers.

The Skirmish of Tippecanoe

All lovely things will have an ending,
All lovely things will fade and die,
And youth, that's now so bravely spending,
Will beg a penny by and by.

All Lovely Things Will Have an Ending
Conrad Aiken

In July of 1952 we had half a dozen Divcos and no taxis—just enough for Fat and Glenn and me. We had lots of experience with Divcos and knew the road, and the trip would be a snap because there wouldn't be any one-way drivers to worry about and the Old Man was on the Coast.

The Divcos were the six-cylinder variety, good for forty-five miles an hour on the level on a calm day. We got it into our heads to make a seven-day trip out of it instead of taking the normal eight or nine days. When we got to Rochester the first day out we didn't make our usual overnight stop, but plugged away for another hour and a quarter—south to Logansport and then west on U.S. 24 to Monticello, a nice-looking burg on the Tippecanoe River. The hotel where we put up charged us four bucks apiece, which was pretty steep for an old country hotel and about twice what the Old Man expected to pay, and he would probably let me hear about it. But the hotel had just repainted the rooms and bought new bedspreads, and they had to get even some way.

It was one of those warm, sticky days. Every time you lifted your arm you broke out in a sweat, and the heat from the engine rolled up through the floorboard of your Divco and almost suffocated you. We felt pretty wrung out and not good for much of anything but beer-drinking, so we had a hamburger and called it dinner and then walked down the main drag to check out the bars.

Certain kinds of experience are no more educational than getting drunk or being bit by horseflies. You swear that you will never let it happen again, because who wants pain or anguish? But a horsefly or a big bender will sneak up on you when your guard is down, and give you the works.

It's the same with hitting a new town. Experience tells you that all small towns are the same—especially that tank towns and whistlestops are the way they are because of the kind of people who live there, and that's the way they like it. But we didn't want to accept that sort of reality, and stuck away in our heads was the hope that some day we would stumble onto a town that would come up to our ideal—a wideopen, catch-as-catch-can town, with a free and friendly girl behind every tree, and more trees than you could count on all your fingers and toes. Not a garish, overpriced town full of raunchy girls—we had already been there—but a peaceful town with lots of nightlife, densely populated with attractive, respectable girls who would hop in the sack with anything on two legs.

Who could tell—maybe Monticello would be that town. Of course we were all too smart to mention such a dumb dream out loud, but that was the main reason we raced through our hamburgers and headed for the taverns. If Monticello should turn out to be the magical town we had long sought, we had best get out there and grab our share before it was all used up or had turned back into a pumpkin. Had we stayed in Rochester, which was like Monticello only bigger, we would have known there was no potential. We would have gone across the street for a bowl of homemade soup and a braunschweiger sandwich, had a couple of bottles of Wiedemann's beer or Drewry's ale, and hit the hay at nine thirty after reading the Chicago papers.

Monticello had three taverns. One was dark, with cobwebs on the windows and a padlock on the door. Another had a sign on the window: FOR MEN ONLY, and was the place where the old geezers from miles around gathered to talk about hog prices and play gin rummy. That left us no choice—gravity dictated that we fall into the last chance. It was a decrepit, high-ceilinged dump smelling of stale beer and ammonia. Dangling from the ceiling were three big old fans, making about forty r.p.m. and not having any effect.

We were the only customers, and it was plain to see that Monticello was a Christian town that would wind up at the bottom of our list—a complete washout. Etiquette required that we buy a round each, and as we poured it down and sweated it out we talked about all the familiar topics: the job and the Old Man and the next trip if there was one and maybe we should get on a union job and what the hell did people *do* in these deadass fuckin' towns to make them think they were still alive and where would we stay the next night, perhaps in Hamilton or Cameron which might just surprise us because any town in Missouri big enough to have a tavern . . . and ain't life hell when you're on the road all the fuckin' time.

Well, whatthehell, you can't win 'em all. We guzzled our beer and got on out of there, feeling virtuous because we were going to get up at four in the morning and make some miles before it got hot. We tightened the towbars on our Divcos and checked the steering cables and safety chains and clearance lights, and while we were doing that a big Packard with some girls in it went by and gave us a toot on the horn and naturally we gave a wave and hollered Hey, come on back—and they made a U-turn and came on back. Just like in the storybooks.

When the Packard with four girls in it pulled up beside our Divcos, Fat, who had a tendency to engage his mouth before putting his brain in gear, said Hey, look at all that meat and no potatoes—and almost queered the deal before it got off the ground. We figured that they were just some of the local talent who had got ahold of their old man's car for the evening, and would have to get home before sundown. They had seen us walking down the street a while earlier and had figured that we were just some of the local hicks with cowshit on our boots. They turned out to be four secretaries from Indianapolis who were taking their two weeks' vacation together and had rented a cottage on Shafer Lake, a couple of miles out of town. The girls were surprised to hear that we were knights of the road rather than haypitching gunsels. We all were so pleased at our unexpected good fortune that we chipped in on a case of beer and headed right out for the cottage.

The broad who owned the car was a female counterpart of Fat—dirty-talking and wanting to get right down to business. By the time we reached the lake they were already swapping spit, and Fat said he didn't think he could get out of the car until he got out of the mood. The tough broad laughed and said she'd slam the door on it, and that would slow him down. The rest of us were embarrassed because Fat and the tough broad were breaking the speed limit, but a couple of beers loosened everybody up and pretty quick we were all getting in the mood—except one of the girls who was sunburned from head to toe and couldn't stand to have anybody touch her, which was okay because there were only three of us guys.

Fat's broad was several years older than the other three, and because she owned the car and was obviously more experienced and less inhibited she tended to be the boss. But after she had got across to us that she could handle men and wouldn't take crap from anybody, she slowed down and reverted to her normal style—a somewhat cruder version of the other three, who were the attractive, respectable girls inexplicably appearing in a deadass small town in Indiana that we had dreamt about but knew we'd never see, because it was impossible.

We didn't have an exaggerated idea of our desirability. We knew that we were underpaid towbar drivers living out of suitcases, without any sharp clothes for disguise or big money to throw around. And how can you make any points if you don't have a false front and a good act?

But the girls treated us like God's gift to women, which would have gone to our heads right now except that we felt the same way about them. Half their vacation had gone by, and they had been kinda down at the mouth because the young executive types and husky college boys they had hoped to meet had put in their appearance somewhere else. Then we fell out of the sky, and the clouds blew away. Life was just one damned thing after another—not all of them bad.

The sun went down across the lake, the evening was hot and humid, the beer was cold and went down easy, and somebody said let's go in for a swim. The girls changed into their bathing suits, and we felt our way down wooden steps to the dock where Glenn and Fat and I stripped to our skivvies. All seven of us boarded a small rowboat, the tough broad rowed out to the middle of the lake, we clutched at each other for a few minutes, then rocked the boat until it tipped over—just the way all seven of us had secretly planned it. We frolicked around for a spell and made luminous splashes and got friendlier faster in the water than we would have on dry land, and Fat said he couldn't get out of the lake until he got out of the mood, and we all laughed. We swam the submerged boat back to the dock, the girls ran up the steps, and Glenn and Fat and I put on our clothes and threw our wet skivvies into the bushes.

The cottage had a main room with two single beds, an antique refrigerator, and a formica table and matching chairs from Sears. There was an alcove off either end of the room, each with a single bed. The alcoves didn't have doors—just heavy curtains—so there wasn't much more privacy than you would have had if you camped in the public square. The sunburned girl was having hot and cold flashes and looked as though she was going to pass out, and one of the other girls said that she would take care of the sunburned one and the two of them disappeared into one of the alcoves—and that's the last we saw of them.

Fat and the tough broad grabbed four beers and took the other alcove, which left me and Glenn and one girl in the main room. She was more my size than Glenn's, and the girl that Glenn had started out with was the one who was playing nursemaid to the sunburned one, which left Glenn with the portable radio and all the beer he could drink. We got some music on the radio to try and liven up the party again. The girl with me, whose name was Esther, would go in for anything short of taking off her clothes, but with Glenn in the same room and the glare of a naked lightbulb and four other people a few feet away she wasn't about to get caught with her pants off, and neither was I—so we opened more beers and got out some cheese and crackers. Fat and his broad started to go at it, and the bedsprings twanged so loudly we were sure they could be heard clear across the lake, and we turned up the volume on the radio so that we wouldn't be embarrassed.

After a while Glenn fell asleep on one of the beds, with a can of beer in his fist and the radio playing music til dawn. Esther and I lay on the other bed, and we fumbled and fiddled with each other for a spell, and soon fell asleep. Every half hour or so we would wake up and play around some more and sip more beer and tell the stories of our lives, and then drop off again. When Glenn woke up he told the story of his life too. Once Fat came out and got two more beers, and sometime after midnight he and the tough broad gave the bedsprings another workout.

Half an hour before sunrise Esther and I went outside and sat on two iron lawn chairs that were wet with dew, and drank the last two beers and looked at the lake and felt the rising sun on our backs and watched the long shadows lying across the damp grass. At sunup the temperature was already seventy-two, and it was going to be another scorcher. I started getting worried about the job, and said that we'd better hit the road for the Coast. I woke up Glenn and Fat, and Esther and the tough broad drove us into town, and bought us breakfast at the corner cafe—which was taking it a notch farther than the storybooks.

We were all trying hard to be congenial and witty, but it was wearing thin because we were feeling rundown from too many beers and not enough sleep. Fat began squirming in his chair, and his broad asked him if he had ants in his pants, and Fat said it sure felt funny without any underwear. When she asked him how come, Fat said that we had thrown our skivvies in the bushes down by the lake, and his broad said Christjesus and Goddamn, they'll throw our ass out of there. She grabbed Fat and swabbed out his throat with her tongue for the last time, and she and Esther promised to write and we promised too and then the girls took off in the Packard.

We went to the hotel to get our suitcases, wishing that we could sack out for a few hours but knowing that we had to get going. Our eyes felt gritty and our mouths tasted like the bottom of a birdcage. We thought it would be one hell of a tough day, but we didn't feel the strain until late afternoon when we were driving right into the sun and had to yell and slap ourselves in the face to stay awake. About every twenty miles we pulled off onto the shoulder, and Glenn and I would get out to stretch. Fat would shut off his engine and slump forward across the steering wheel to sleep. We'd give him five minutes and then make him get out and walk around until he was able to drive again. He looked pretty bad and moaned and groaned a lot, but when we kidded him and asked him if it had been worth it he got a big shiteating grin on his face and said it was the best time he'd had since Christ was a corporal.

We plugged along until seven thirty and got to Monroe City, Missouri, which put us on the normal schedule for Divcos, but we had to give up the idea of making a seven-day trip out of it. By the time we checked into the hotel and washed up we had our second wind, and went to the tavern to have a few cold ones to settle the dust. We were long on endurance in those days. Never say die.

That night in Monticello, Glenn got to thinking about how badly he wanted to quit the road and settle down. Three nights later when we stayed in Las Vegas he popped the question to Flora, and that was the beginning of the end for him. Esther and I exchanged letters twice, but I couldn't see that I was ever going to get to Indianapolis, or that she was ever going to get away from there, and that was the end of that.

Fat said you could never tell about that strange stuff. He sweated it out for the next nine days, and when he didn't come down with a dose of the clap it took a big load off his mind and left him with nothing but fond memories.

Between Past and Future

> Where is it, this present? It has melted in our grasp, fled ere we could touch it, gone in the instant of becoming.
>
> ***The Principles of Psychology***
> **William James**

One cold morning in 1953 we headed west out of Albuquerque on U.S. 66 with a flock of taxis. The temperature was near zero, and with no heaters in the cars we were about to freeze our feet. We made a stop at the King Café, between Laguna Pueblo and San Fidel, to thaw out.

The King Café had a couple of gas pumps, and sold junk jewelry and rotten food to the tourists. It was run by a man in his middle fifties who was there in self-imposed exile. He said that during prohibition he had had a bootlegging run from Kalamazoo to Chicago Heights, and had made so many enemies that he had to stay away from that part of the country. He was working himself to death because he couldn't get a white man or woman to work for him way out there, and he was putting in sixteen hours a day. The only help he could get was an Indian girl who was willing enough but couldn't make change or cook white man's food.

He made an offer to any one of us who was interested: free room and board and a fourth of the profits, in exchange for manning the gas pumps and repairing tires seventy-two hours a week. And to show that his heart was in the right place, he would throw in the Indian girl as a bonus. She didn't look like much and didn't speak English worth a damn, but she could fuck like a rabbit and she never said no.

On a zero morning with your feet so cold it made tears run down your cheeks, the thought of getting inside by the fire and going a couple of fast rounds with a hot-natured squaw was almost enough to make you kiss the Old Man goodbye right on the spot. Ed and Red actually sounded interested, and they told the ex-bootlegger that they would think it over and stop by to see him on the way east. Of course once their feet were warm and their balls were no longer in an uproar, they thought better of it.

Most of the drivers expressed at least a passing interest in getting married and settling down, even those who had tried married life on for size and found that it didn't fit. Red had tried it for a few years just after the war and thought that it had been going along in good style—except for when his old lady had the monthlies and got mean and nasty and he had to slap her down—until one day, without any warning, she hit him from behind with a cast-iron skillet. The blow left him with a split ear, a mild concussion, and a strong desire to put a lot of mileage between himself and his old lady. He had been managing a market in Grand Rapids, with an assured future because it was a big chain outfit and the sky was the limit for an honest hardworker, and maybe he could have become regional manager. But the cast-iron skillet knocked that crap out of his head, and he went on the road to get away from it all.

Red was smart enough to learn from experience, and he never wanted to get hitched again. He preferred to take it on the fly, with no strings attached and no questions asked—and if in doubt, don't give your right name. Whenever Red talked about maybe—sometime—having a more settled life, he mentioned only the benefits—some good home cooking and a steady piece, but he never talked about duties and responsibilities because he wasn't interested in those things. For the time being—which might as easily as not be the rest of his life—Red was content to live out of a suitcase and drive over the road for the Old Man.

Few of the men had permanent addresses. In the nearly ten years that I worked for the Old Man, I was the only one of his drivers who voted in an election. Most of them were never counted in a census, and thus did not exist statistically—unless they filed for unemployment or in some other way encountered a bureaucracy. Their financial transactions were entirely on a cash basis. No one had a checking account, nor could see any reason for having one. No one had a savings account, because they had nothing to save.

Living out of a suitcase wasn't just an expression, it was the reality. I traveled with a cheap, metal-covered suitcase, the sort of thing that could be bought for five dollars in an Army-Navy surplus store. One would last a year or two, and when the hinges broke you threw it away and bought another. I always had a batch of clothes in a laundry in Los Angeles and another batch in a laundry in Detroit, so that at either end of the trip I could blossom forth in clean khakis and sport shirt. Most of the men had with them all their worldly possessions: some clothing, a razor and toothbrush, perhaps some basic tools, and that was it. The only reality was the immediate moment—the place where you were, the things you carried with you, today's activity. The past was composed of fragments that could not be put together to form a coherent memory or to provide a clue as to what you might expect from life. The future was the evening's entertainment and, at most, the prospects for the next week or two. Life was just one damned thing after another, with no indication of what the next thing would be.

It was scarcely possible to think of a time "after the Old Man." Although the Old Man's business was erratic, that didn't matter too much. Nobody in his right mind wanted to work all the time anyway. A little vacation now and then did you good, just so it didn't drag out to where you were getting hungry and cold. When the Old Man laid us off temporarily, most of us stayed in L.A. It was a better town than Detroit, and sometimes it was possible to hire out by the day to load furniture vans—the furniture haulers stayed in the same hotel as we did, the El Rey at Sixth and San Pedro.

If we went back to Detroit, the only chance for work was to hang around at Spink's and hope that they could use you on the crew that picked up cars and brought them back to the lot. Spink had a half-ton panel truck equipped with two wooden benches in back. Six or eight men would go to Plymouth or Dodge Main or Divco or the Dodge truck plant, and bring back single vehicles, or perhaps take some cars down to the docks on the Detroit River to be loaded on boats for Cleveland or Buffalo. Spink paid union scale, and it was easy work compared to what we normally did, but it had the drawback of all easy work—there wasn't much of it. Once when several of us were working on pickup for Spink, a business agent for Local 299 came around to check dues books to see that everybody was paid up. When he found these non-union men who said they worked on a trip-fee basis he thought he was on to something big, and threatened to close Spink down. I persuaded him to call the union office, and they reamed him out good and told him to get his fucking ass out of there and not to fuck around in matters that weren't his fucking business. Whatever the deal was between Hoffa and the Old Man, it worked. There were no advantages to it, except that it kept the union off our backs. As far as we could make out, the Teamsters Union was a money-grubbing outfit. The big wheels in the union had a pile of money to play with, and though we had no idea what games they played we were dead sure that they were a bunch of crooks. Along in the middle fifties we were pleased to hear that Frank Collins, the secretary-treasurer of Local 299, got sent up for perjury. We didn't know what else he might have been guilty of, but figured that he deserved to be in jail for some reason or other. We favored putting those guys in jail even if they weren't guilty.

In a way it was our own fault that we were caught between the Old Man and the union. If you're willing to work cheap, there is bound to be someone who will pop up and take advantage of you. But we had no attractive alternatives. Jacking up the Old Man for higher wages would have run him out of business—or else he'd throw you away and hire someone else—and you'd be out in the cold. All things considered, it was better to keep working for low wages on a job you liked than to be sitting on the shelf because you were too proud to be screwed. Several times a year we would get all wound up about the trip fee, but there was nothing to be done, and we only made ourselves angry and frustrated. If we had been financially independent we could have told the Old Man what to do with his one-horse business, or if we had had families and homes we could have gone home and cussed our wives and kicked our dogs, but as it was we invariably had to resort to the Heroic Treatment. We went to the nearest bar, bought beer, gulped it down, then cried into the empty glasses. And after a while we felt better.

In the early fifties we felt good most of the time, or at least those of us who were still young and carefree did. We might bitch and gripe about the job now and then, but that was just to keep our hand in. We could drink most of the night and drive all day and then do it again, and we never seemed to run down. The older men were plagued by ulcers and piles and fading vision and falling hair and a sense that the years were running away. They worried about money and health, and cherished their possessions, and talked about Social Security, and dreamed about the end of the future.

We young guys didn't worry at all. We didn't own a thing for moth and rust to corrupt, nor thieves break through and steal. There was money enough to satisfy our needs, time enough to do everything in the world, unquestioning optimism about the future. Life was open-ended, and everything was possible.

One Nation, Indivisible

America, my country, is almost a
Continent and hardly yet a nation.
Patria Mia
Ezra Pound

The Old Man began his driveaway business before that line of endeavor was regulated by the I.C.C. When the I.C.C. issued permits the Old Man got grandfather rights, which restricted him to what he had already been doing—transporting new cars and trucks from Detroit and South Bend to Los Angeles. But it made the Old Man angry to be regulated at all, by anybody. He had been getting along just fine without the I.C.C.

If the Old Man had been born a generation or two earlier he would have made a great Robber Baron. He believed that anyone with gumption and initiative would rightfully get ahead, as long as the government and the liberal professors who had never met a payroll would keep their hands off. America was a wonderful country and all men were born free and equal—and then you were on your own, and may the best man win. You could charge what the traffic would bear, undercut your competitors, and squeeze your employees, because that was the nature of business. "Life is governed by the rules of fair play and the discipline of the marketplace"—which meant no holds barred.

As they taught you way back in grade school, the U.S. of A. was all one big country; and in high school you learned that it was the absence of tariff barriers that helped to make the country rich and strong. But when you were driving in interstate commerce, crossing a state line was like entering a foreign country.

The Old Man used Indiana transport plates for his vehicles, because they were cheaper than Michigan plates. The law required that the Old Man have a place of business in Indiana, so he maintained the fiction that he had an office in Rochester—but the address was the Karn Hotel, and if any mail came it was forwarded to the Old Man in California. Michigan and Illinois didn't care what sort of plates were on a vehicle, because they issued transport plates too and wanted them to be accepted by other states. But once you crossed the Mississippi the trouble began.

Missouri sold annual driveaway permits for twenty-five dollars, and each driver had to carry one to to show to the state cops and the guys at the scales. When we crossed into Kansas we mailed our Missouri permits back to Barney's filling station in Havana, Illinois, for the use of the next convoy coming through.

Kansas had a Port of Entry that was the next thing to a customs house and passport control. You filled out a lengthy form, put Kansas Corporation Commission plates on your vehicles, and got a sticker with a big letter K to put on your windshield. They sent the Old Man a quarterly bill, but I never did know what it cost. The Ports of Entry were partly a political patronage deal—it was nice to have all those jobs to pass out.

Colorado charged on a ton-mile basis: so many vehicles times so many pounds each times the 185 miles we were in the state gave you the number of pounds of iron we were transporting, and multiplying that figure by a three-place decimal gave you the amount of money the Old Man had to pay Colorado for the wear and tear on its roads.

The moneygrubbing state of New Mexico didn't rely on fancy formulas—they wanted cash on the barrelhead, or you couldn't turn a wheel on the potholed roads in their state. The tariff was seven dollars and fifty cents for every driven vehicle, and five dollars for every towed or carried vehicle.

Arizona couldn't even admit to itself that it was charging an arbitrary fee for vehicles in transit. For the first six months of the year it cost four fifty for every vehicle with wheels on the ground, and in the second six months it was three dollars. To disguise what they were doing they called it temporary registration, but of course they had no intention of ever issuing license plates. Instead, they gave us big red cards to stick on our windshields, which we had to turn in at the inspection station at Ehrenberg just before we left the state. We couldn't make bad jokes about it to the guys in the inspection stations, because they were mighty thin-skinned and didn't want to admit that part of what they were doing to pass away the years was pure bullshit.

California had the moneymakingest deal of all: the Department of Motor Vehicles had dreamed up what was called a "caravan permit." There was a charge of fifteen dollars on every new or used vehicle brought into the state for sale or resale, and it didn't matter whether they were driven, towed, or carried—you had to shell out for every one. It was such a good moneymaker that it was extended to cover vehicles being transported between the northern and southern parts of the state, with the dividing line near Bakersfield.

The Old Man was plenty disgusted with New Mexico and Arizona for charging such high fees and providing narrow, rough, high-crowned roads to drive on. Even when they built new roads they weren't any good—rough the day they were opened, and full of holes inside of six months. The road surfaces seemed to consist of sand scraped up from along the right of way, mixed with waste oil, spread on the roadbed, and given the once-over-lightly with an underweight steamroller—which produced a surface fit for a driveway.

Nothing made the Old Man hotter than caravan permits. They made him so hot that in the late forties he sued the state of California. Eight years later he won the suit. Caravan permits were declared illegal, and California had to cough up a lot of money to the Old Man—about eighty-five thousand dollars. The Old Man lit up a Corona Corona, and was in a mellow mood for quite some time.

The third year I drove for the Old Man we changed our route when we went east by car. Instead of exactly retracing the route when on our way west—north from Albuquerque to Raton, across southeast Colorado, and into Kansas on U.S. 50—we stayed on 66 to Tucumcari, then cut northeast on U.S. 54 through the Texas and Oklahoma panhandles, into Kansas at Liberal and back on our regular route at Hutchinson. It was a shorter route and had less hill-climbing, but the Old Man had sworn that he would never again operate through Texas ever since Texas had screwed him out of a lot of money before the war.

It was along about 1938, when the Old Man was moving several thousand Studebakers and Hudsons a year. He operated on the southern route, crossing the river at Cape Girardeau, and going down to Blytheville, Little Rock, and Texarkana. It wasn't the most direct route, but after the first three days there was little chance of getting snowed on—and for the sake of convenience the Old Man went that way year around.

From Texarkana he went clear across the state to El Paso, which was close to 800 miles. Unknown to the Old Man, the Texas Railroad Commission—which regulated the railroads and trucking and oil production, and perhaps the whole state—had felt frustrated because the Old Man and other driveaway outfits were getting off scot-free. The commission pressured the state legislature into passing a stiff law that would sock it to the Old Man. On the day it was passed, the governor signed it into law—and it became effective immediately.

The Old Man had three caravans in Texas at the time: one in Texarkana, another a hundred miles west of there at Sulphur Springs, and the third at Weatherford, twenty-five miles west of Fort Worth. In the middle of the night the state cops came pounding on the door of the pilot with the caravan in Texarkana, demanding to know if he had the permits that had been authorized by law just that day. Of course the pilot had never heard of any such thing, and when he said "What permits?" they hauled him off to the hoosegow for being in violation of the law. But even Texas is still in the U.S. of A., and while they were robbing you blind they couldn't help but make a feeble stab at trying to make it look open and above board. Being law-abiding and decent types, the cops let the pilot make the usual one phone call, so he called the Old Man in L.A. The Old Man called the pilots of the other two caravans and told them to wake up their drivers and hit the road and get on out of Texas. The caravan in Sulphur Springs headed north, but the cops caught them in Paris and put them in jail. The caravan at Weatherford, with Buschbacher as pilot, headed north on back roads in the early morning darkness and got into Oklahoma undetected. Then they headed northwest and crossed the Texas panhandle on farm roads, and made it all the way to Tucumcari, New Mexico by evening.

The Railroad Commission made the Old Man's pilots buy permits for the two caravans they'd caught, and fined them for not already having the permits. To top it off, the Old Man had to pay twenty dollars a head to get his drivers out of jail. The whole rotten deal cost the Old Man more than two thousand dollars, and he never operated in Texas again. Just hearing the name of Texas made the Old Man angry. His favorite joke was: **Directions to Texas: Go east til you smell it, then south til you step in it.** It always made the Old Man feel good to tell that to someone who hadn't heard it before.

When we started going east through the Texas and Oklahoma panhandles, I mentioned to the Old Man that I thought it was a better route: good roads, about a hundred miles shorter, easier grades, and a lower average gasoline price. At first the Old Man wasn't interested, and when I said "Texas" he said to watch my language. But I mentioned it a couple of more times in the next six months, and the Old Man decided to look into it.

On one of the trips east we stayed on U.S. 66 and went to Oklahoma City, where I checked with the Corporation Commission. They were like Kansas—required OCC plates on the vehicles and charged on a ton-mile basis, which for a driveaway operation wouldn't amount to much. The Old Man wrote to the Railroad Commission in Austin. They informed him that they too charged on a ton-mile basis, and that special permits for driveaway no longer existed. But even though the Old Man had it in writing he didn't believe it. He was dead sure that the rotten state of Texas was trying to sucker him in, and once he got his convoys in Texas again they would lower the boom on him.

The Old Man was torn both ways, because on paper it looked as though he could save money by changing that part of the route. In the end it was his hatred of Texas that won out; we didn't make the change. It sure bothered him to miss out on a chance to save some bucks, so one day when we were talking it over I gave him—by way of consolation—a new one about Texas. Texans are inordinately proud of the Alamo, so if a Texan should ever ask you if you've heard of the Alamo, you say **Yes, that's the place where two thousand Texans fought a battle against a drunken Indian and two pregnant Mexicans—and lost.**

The Old Man liked that one so much that he gave it equal billing with **Directions to Texas.**

Defender of Freedom

And but for these vile guns,
He would himself have been a soldier.
Henry IV
William Shakespeare

The Old Man himself often went on the road until 1954. Whenever we had enough taxis for two crews, the Old Man would fly or ride the Super Chief, while the rest of us beat our way across the country by car. He and I would each run a convoy, usually operating a day apart with the Old Man going first because he had to be in L.A. to pay off my crew when we arrived. It was strictly a one-man business, run out of an office in the back of the Old Man's house—not even a secretary to open the mail and answer the phone. The Old Man carried the business around in his head and his briefcase, and if he had suddenly died it would have died with him.

The Old Man liked it that way. He was the boss, and he didn't have to answer to anyone. After I had been on the job for a couple of years he would sometimes solicit my opinion, but when we disagreed about anything connected with the job he had the final say-so—even when he was wrong. Once when he got to reminiscing about before the war, the Old Man said that he and his two brothers got along just fine, so long as they stayed away from each other and worked on their own. The Old Man was the top dog, while Carl ran caravans and Andrew operated an office in Chicago where he hired one-way drivers to be sent to South Bend by bus.

The Old Man thought that any business owned by equal partners was bound to run onto the rocks. Somebody had to be the big boss, else sooner or later there would be competition, conflicting ideas about methods of operation, and arguments over money. It was the money that would kill your business. One of the partners would scrimp and save and pinch pennies, and the other would raid the petty-cash drawer and want to live high—and might eventually steal from the company. And then one partner would sue the other, and it would wreck the business and finish off the friendship. Just thinking about such a sad end made the Old Man depressed and philosophical.

"You know, Pete," he said. "The heart of the capitalist tragedy is when you are in litigation against your partner."

I thought that was a profound remark, but I didn't know whether the Old Man was quoting someone or had thought it up himself—he didn't say. It sounded like what Karl Marx would have said if he had been half owner of a small business and had caught his partner with his hand in the till. It was such a choice remark that I passed it on to some of the other guys on the job as an example of the depth and essential humanity of the Old Man. They weren't much impressed. Someone laughed because he thought I was making a joke, and Freeman Morse shrugged and said, "If you're in a bind like that it's your own fucking fault."

That was less tragic than the Old Man's vision of life, but more profound. Freeman had a clear view of what went on in the world. Some things were done to you, some things you did to or for yourself, and some things just happened. Clearly, being in business with the wrong partner was in the second category.

Although Freeman sneered at the virtues of sobriety and hard work—as espoused and practiced by such as Glenn Miles—he was himself a hardworking, hustling, resourceful man who could always find work when he wanted it. He had once tried drawing unemployment, but found it both demeaning and boring. He was sometimes a low-pressure con man, and wasn't beyond a bit of dishonesty when the opportunity occurred—but he didn't try to create opportunities. He was strictly honest with his friends, and though he wasn't always sober he was reliable on the job. A want of sobriety was common enough, and Freeman never let his drinking interfere with his work—and the other way around, too. Life was meant to be enjoyed and was not to be confused with work, which was merely the means to the end.

Freeman was good-natured but hotheaded. His method of dealing with an unpleasant or frustrating situation was either to overwhelm it with a great burst of energy or to walk off and leave it; and when up against an unpleasant or difficult person, Freeman would either laugh in his face or hit him one right in the mouth. If you didn't like your circumstances or companions, you either left them or smashed them into shape. Life was too short to waste any of it being indecisive or doing what you didn't want to do.

One of a convoy pilot's chores was to fill out the I.C.C. logbook, and to see that the other drivers kept their logbooks up to date. It was my custom to have the drivers fill out their logs after we were installed in the hotel for the night, when they came around to get their daily three-dollar draw. Almost all of the drivers were on the draw even if they had plenty of money in their pockets, on the theory that it was a good idea to stay well ahead.

One evening Freeman protested this routine as an infringement of his rights, saying that he was full-grown and didn't want to be treated that way. I said Fill out the logbook now, and Freeman said No and I said Yes and he said Hell no and I said Fill it out now or no daily draw, and Freeman said Go fuck yourself, and stomped out of the room. Two minutes later he was in good humor again, telling jokes and laughing and cutting up, and you would never have known that he was mad enough to beat the bejesus out of me. We all went out together and had dinner and a few beers, so it was plain that Freeman hadn't needed the draw.

A year later it looked as though the Selective Service System was about to select Freeman. His draft board in Tennessee had kept after him, and despite his nomadic life and lack of a permanent address had managed to track him down, and had his papers transferred to a board in L.A. They tested him and found that he was bright enough to do whatever the army had in mind for him, and pronounced him in fine physical condition. A date was set for Freeman's induction, and soon there were going to be more infringements of Freeman's rights than he ever could have imagined.

The draft board timed Freeman's departure for the army so as to let him make two more trips. He was to be inducted the day after we arrived in L.A. on the second trip, and we had a rousing sendoff party at the Circle B—all of us laughing louder and drinking faster than usual. I left the party at midnight, after shaking hands with Freeman and wishing him luck and telling him not to let the army fuck him over. A furniture van driver on an adjacent stool overheard, and advised Freeman not to let the army shit on him, and Freeman grinned and said he wouldn't, and the furniture guy said Just open your mouth, and Freeman knocked the guy off the stool onto the floor and kicked him in the stomach, and when the guy vomited all over the floor the bartender threw him out for messing up the place.

Freeman said he wasn't too sure he would like the army, and Fat—the old soldier—said you could do two years standing on your head, and just remember: Don't volunteer for anything, and you'll have it made in the shade. You better believe it.

I went back to the hotel by myself, leaving Freeman and the others still going full blast at the Circle B. About four o'clock there was a tremendous pounding on my door. It was Freeman, sounding drunk and maudlin, saying that he was going off to throw the blocks to the Commies and might never see me again, and he wanted to say goodbye one last time.

I couldn't persuade him to go away. He was making so much noise that I was afraid the hotel management would get after us, so I groggily got out of bed and opened the door. Freeman charged in swinging both hands, knocking me back onto the bed and jumping on top of me and trying to bash my face in. I was too stunned to put up much of a defense, but Freeman was too drunk to do much damage. After a few seconds of Freeman throwing ineffectual punches while I shouted Stop it you dumb crazy drunken sonofabitch, Freeman stopped, and started to laugh like crazy. I got up, closed the door, and put on my skivvies and shoes. When a man has on his skivvies and shoes, he's better prepared to handle social situations.

I asked Freeman why he was trying to beat me up, and Freeman said he couldn't remember, and that he was surprised at himself because he had always liked me even though I had my nose stuck in a book too much and didn't drink bourbon and was growing old before my time because I took life too seriously. I said that if I was going to run convoys I had to take it seriously or else we would never get anywhere, and that reminded Freeman of why he wanted to clobber me: it was that incident about filling out the logbook or no three bucks, which had stuck in his craw for a year. I gave him half an apology for that, but said that I still thought it was right and necessary and that if he ever got to be a convoy leader he would see what I meant, and Freeman guffawed and said that was a fat fucking chance. I said that it was a mite peculiar that he hadn't tried to beat me up until the night before he went to the army, and Freeman said that he hadn't lost all his marbles—if he had tried it earlier I would have fired him.

We shot the breeze for a spell about the world and life, and Freeman suddenly blurted out What happened to my beer? We looked all over but couldn't find it. Then Freeman remembered that he had put it down so that he'd have both hands free to clobber me. We opened the door, and there was his six-pack sitting in the hall. The beer improved the quality of our conversation considerably, and we were getting on like the best of friends when suddenly there was another tremendous pounding on my door. It was Ben Kuhel, saying that it was an emergency and he had to get in. This time I was wide awake and much more cautious. I stuck my shoe against the door, and sure enough—when I unlocked it Ben tried to burst in. I said Nothing doing, but Ben said that he had come to warn me that that nogood ridgerunner Freeman was coming over to beat me up, and if I would let him in he would hide behind the door and when Freeman showed up we would both jump him and beat the piss out of him.

So I let Ben in, and when he saw Freeman he almost dropped his teeth. Ben had a pint of bourbon. His plan had been for the two of us to drink the bourbon and then use the empty bottle to coldcock Freeman. But I didn't drink bourbon and Freeman was already there and all was peace and harmony. So Ben and Freeman had the bourbon with beer chasers, and I worked away on another beer, and Freeman told about being second cook in the merchant marine—which was the only other kind of work he had ever done steady—and Ben told some stories about driving for Kenosha Auto Transport in the thirties, and every story had a bottle in it somewhere.

At six o'clock the sun was coming up and the beer and bourbon were gone. When Ben had been drinking whiskey his breath smelled so bad you were sure that something had crawled down his throat and died, and I thought I might be sick before I could persuade him that the party was over and he should go to his own room and pass out for the day. Even Freeman, whose senses were badly dulled, noticed the stench, and said Goddamit Ben, you got breath like an open sewer, and they almost had a fight but I kept saying "the army, the army, Freeman's going to the army," and Ben said if Freeman was going off to defend freedom then it was plain the whole country was going to hell on horseback, and Freeman said he was going out to make the world safe for women, children, and towbar drivers. They went down the hall together, laughing like crazy.

Seven or eight months later Freeman showed up at the Mount Royal Hotel in Detroit. He was wearing civilian clothes, and we thought he was on leave. We asked him how he liked the army, and he said he wasn't in the army and never had been. He had dutifully gone to the Union Station that morning in L.A., where he met the recruiting sergeant who was shipping off a contingent of twenty men. Freeman hadn't had any sleep, and was so drunk he couldn't walk straight and was barely coherent. The sergeant checked everybody's gear to see that they had their toilet articles and a change of underwear and socks.

Freeman didn't have any of those things. In his overnight bag he had a dozen half-pints of whiskey and thirty Mexican wristwatches, which he was going to sell—at enormous profit—to the greenhorns in basic training. The sergeant canceled Freeman on the spot, and the draft board reclassified him because there was some concern that he was an alcoholic. After the big sendoff we'd given him, Freeman was too embarrassed to come back right away to make more trips for the Old Man. He went down to San Pedro and signed on as second cook on a United Fruit Company ship, and went back and forth to Central America, hauling bananas, until he was tired of it and wanted to go back driving.

We were doing a lot of business, and I took him on. The second night of the trip we stayed in Shelbina, Missouri. The other crew, including Ben Kuhel, was going east, and stopped to hobnob for a spell before driving on to Detroit. Freeman was upstairs in his room, reading a magazine. When Ben heard that Freeman was back on the job, he snuck up the stairs and, without warning, burst into the room. He neither looked at Freeman nor said anything to him, but rushed over to the washbasin, unzipped his pants, pissed into the washbasin, zipped up, rushed out of the room and down the stairs and got in the car and took off for Detroit. When Freeman learned that it had really been Ben and not an apparition he joined in the laughter. He was just as ready to enjoy a joke on himself as on someone else.

Several months later the Old Man needed another pilot to run convoys, and Freeman was elected because he had made the most trips. He enjoyed the higher wage he got for being pilot, but the responsibility didn't do him any good. He became even more short-tempered, and mean and nasty to boot. He didn't laugh as much and hardly enjoyed life at all and worried about the heartburn he had all the time that maybe was an ulcer or worse, and wondered if maybe working too hard didn't give you cancer. He was ready to tell the Old Man to take the pilot's job and shove it, because it didn't pay half enough for a white man to put up with all that crap.

After Freeman's third trip as pilot he was on his way east and met me in Kansas as I was going west with a convoy. We stopped beside the road and chatted for half an hour. Freeman complained about the difficulties of running a convoy and getting the drivers to do what he wanted—in particular, keeping their logbooks up to date. But he had found a way: "If they don't fill out their fuckin' logs I don't give them any fuckin' money." And I said That's right, Freeman, that's the way you gotta handle it. Freeman laughed like crazy, and we never said anything else about that issue.

Ed's Golden Girl

> I see young men . . . whose misfortune it is to have inherited farms, houses, barns, cattle, and farming tools; for these are more easily acquired than got rid of . . . . The portionless, who struggle with no such unnecessary inherited encumbrances, find it labor enough to subdue and cultivate a few cubic feet of flesh.
>
> ***Walden***
>
> **Henry David Thoreau**

What was wrong with life was the country itself. It was too vast, too diverse, too extreme—and promised more than there was. The first time around was a ball. You thought that the whole country was yours for the asking, and your first concern was to dip right in and get your fair share. But it would pour through your fingers, giving you a big kick and a fading memory—and never anything that lasted long enough to be nailed down.

It was a nonstop country. To get what it offered you had to get off your duff and start out—and once having set yourself in motion, there was no stopping. If at first you didn't find whatever it was that you thought you wanted, the only thing to do was to step up the pace. But if that was the answer, how come the Old Man was still running so hard when he was pushing seventy? The idea was that if you had space and time enough it was possible to do anything, but it didn't pan out that way. There was too little time and the country had no limits, and we went through life like a dose of salts—and life would soon be all cleaned out. And you might wind up as a bum, or perhaps like the Old Man—with gangrene of the soul, and able to think only of money.

Life was money, and money was life, and you had to think about money whether you had made your pile or didn't have a dime. But for us there was an in-between place, a state where we were working steady and eating good and had a new shirt and enough folding money to get out and kick around. There was no rent to pay, no bills coming in, and we were contemptuous of all those people who were weighed down by their possessions and were obliged to keep on sweating for fear they would miss a payment and it would all be taken away. Only when we had just *some* money—but not too much—were we free from having to think about money.

Ed, like the others, blew his dough in as soon as he was paid. Sometimes he would send a money order to one of his sisters in Detroit, as a form of thanks for past meals and use of the couch and as pre-payment for the next time he was laid off and needed a place to stay. But the rabbits and the beerjoints got the better part of Ed's cash. He never thought about the future—perhaps because he didn't think there was a future. And he was probably right.

In the spring of 1955, after many months of arguing and coaxing, I convinced Ed that he should start a savings account as insurance against a rainy day. Ed was then thirty-eight years old, and had never had a savings account or checking account. The only times he ever saw the insides of a bank were when he walked uptown to the Bank of California main office on Spring Street and cashed the Old Man's paychecks.

Ed was suspicious of banks, and wanted to know what they would do with his money once he had deposited it. I tried to convey my limited knowledge of how banks employed their funds, but it didn't sound good to Ed. What counted with Ed were the visible effects of banking activity—swanky new bank buildings, and the bankers driving Cadillacs. As a selling point I told Ed that the bank would pay interest on his deposits. Ed wanted to know where the bank got the money to pay the interest, and when I explained that the bank lent out large sums of money at higher interest than it paid, Ed said that sounded like a license to steal. He was probably right about that, too. What finally sold Ed on starting a savings account was the argument that if he got a couple of hundred bucks ahead he could hit the date harvest festival in Indio—where he had been wanting to go ever since 1937—and do it up in style.

Ed opened an account in the bank on the corner next to the El Rey Hotel. He put in twenty-five dollars, and when all he had to show for it was a passbook *saying* that he had twenty-five dollars—rather than having the money in his pocket—he said he felt worried and a bit foolish, as though he had been done out of his dough by a sharper. When Ed was paid off at the end of a trip I walked up to the Bank of California with him, and then stuck to him like glue and marched him back to the bank by the El Rey and waited while he deposited another twenty-five smackers in his growing account. If it wasn't done that way, Ed might stop in a bar uptown, just to have one. But he'd have two or three, and then he'd stop in at the Circle B where he'd meet some of the other guys—and that would be all she wrote.

When Ed's bank balance hit the magical figure of one hundred dollars he suddenly became mighty proud of his thrifty habits, and he made deposits voluntarily. Like anyone with a growing fortune he dreamed about a rosy future, and began to dream out loud about murky plans for a complete overhaul of his life. He would salt his money away until he had enough saved up to make a fresh start—say, an even thousand, which would give him a cushion for when he quit the Old Man, and was looking around for a good job. Given time, he was bound to land something—perhaps driving city delivery for a freight outfit, or a route for a wholesale drug house—and if he needed more money to tide him over until the right job came along he could always go hacking for Yellow Cab. He would get a nice studio or one-bedroom apartment all his own—maybe out in West L.A., but anyhow well away from the lousy atmosphere of Sixth and San Pedro, and the Circle B, and the other crummy bars where he always blew his money in and got all fucked up. And once he had the right job and the right place to live, it just naturally followed that he would meet the right woman.

As he looked ahead to a brighter future, Ed occasionally patronized higher-caliber bars—as if to get in shape for moving upward in society. Soon he was telling us about this woman he'd met at the Glass Hat Bar in the Hayward Hotel. She was a goodlooker and strictly class—totally unlike the B-girls and barflies we usually met. This woman lived right there in the Hayward, and eventually it came out that she was temporarily working as a cocktail waitress—but she was really cut out for better things. She had good secretarial skills and A-one references, and was too proud to take a permanent job that was beneath her. She could see the potential in Ed, too, and probably just to bolster his ego she swallowed some of her pride and let him play the role of provider—some good booze and a couple of sacks of groceries every time he came to town.

We thought there was something fishy about it, but Ed was still salting away twenty-five a trip—and if he hadn't been spending the rest of his money on this woman he would have pissed it away in the bars. We never got to see his woman, because Ed said that she was too highclass to be hanging around with a bunch of down-at-the-heels towbar drivers, and Freeman said that if her shit didn't stink she should get her ass gold-plated. That made Ed mad, but if he had tried to fight Freeman he would have been whipped, so he held his water. Freeman was much taken with his own wit, and after that he always asked Ed how was the girl with the gold-plated ass—and then he laughed like crazy.

When Ed got his savings account to two hundred and fifty dollars he couldn't stand the burden of his wealth. Five minutes after the deposit that put it at that record high, he went back to the bank and withdrew fifty—a fifty-dollar bill, because he liked the picture of U.S. Grant. He said that he was just trying it out to see if withdrawals worked as well as deposits, and that he would put it back tomorrow. But he went uptown and spent twenty-two dollars on a bag of fancy imported foods and a fifth of Old Grand-Dad—which was his golden girl's taste—to surprise her because she didn't think he was due in town for a couple of days yet.

He let himself into her room with his own key, and surprised her in the sack with one of the hotel desk clerks. Ed got the picture right away: the gold was brass, and he had only been a meal ticket. He broke the whiskey bottle in the shower and dumped the imported food on the bed and announced that she would never see him again because it was plain that she didn't appreciate his true worth and honorable intentions. She got haughty and said what kind of a girl did he think she was that he could buy her devotion with a bag of cheap food from a supermarket, and Ed said, "Sis on you, pister, you ain't so mucking fuch"—and he got out while he was ahead.

Ed went on a bender that night that broke all previous records, and wound up with a two-bit whore who rolled him for every dime he had. At three in the morning he was wending his way down Sixth Street like a wobbly duck, and when he was only two blocks from the El Rey the drunk patrol picked him up and hauled him out to the Lincoln Heights jail and threw him in the tank with the skidrow bums. He called me the next day at noon, and I went over and paid the fifteen dollars to get him out.

Four of us were leaving that afternoon for Detroit. I hustled Ed back to the hotel so that he could clean up and check out. He kept saying that he didn't want to make more trips, but he always said that when he was drunk or hungover so I paid no attention. It was February. Back in Detroit were gray skies and cold winds and slush. In L.A. the sun was shining and you could walk down the street in shirtsleeves. Ed said he couldn't stand the thought of freezing his balls any more, and I insisted that he had to do it because he didn't have a job in L.A. and it would be a dumb stunt to lay around and burn up the dough that he'd saved over a stretch of five or six months. Ed was unshaven and his clothes were wrinkled and he had vomit on his shoes and he said he felt so sick he wouldn't be able to stand the ride east in a car. Freeman got an eyeful of Ed and said that he looked like he'd been hit with a blivet—which is ten pounds of shit in a five-pound bag.

After a shower and shave, with clean clothes and shoes, and some toast and fruit juice which was all he could get down, Ed looked better. He looked like he'd been sick for a month and had just got out of the hospital. What bothered him most was losing his money to the whore. A screwing like that, he said, and I didn't even get kissed. He said he was too sick to go east, but we threw his suitcase in the trunk and shoved him into the back seat—and in five minutes he was snoring with his mouth open.

At sunset we were rolling down Whitewater grade into the desert. We stopped at Indio for supper, stopped at Blythe for gas, and stopped for coffee at the Ranch House Café at the top of the hill at Yarnell after we had come up out of the desert. Ed slept through all of it. He didn't come to until we were on the fifteen miles of winding mountain road going into Prescott, where each curve to the right banged his head against the window. He had been out for eight hours. He was surprised to find himself in a car, and wanted to know where we were and what was going on. The last thing he could remember was having toast and fruit juice in L.A., and he thought we were kidding him about being almost to Prescott—until he got his eyes focused and could see patches of snow gleaming in the moonlight among the trees. He said emphatically that he didn't want to make any more trips, and he was sure sorry if it screwed up me or the Old Man but he was going back to L.A. We couldn't talk him out of it. We stopped at our usual place, the Vendome Hotel, and Ed took his suitcase out of the car. He was flat broke, so I lent him a twenty to tide him over.

When we arrived in L.A. on the next trip we found Ed flat broke again and pearldiving at a hashhouse on Fifth Street to keep from starving. He had stayed overnight at the Vendome, and then rode the Trailways back to L.A. He yanked the whole two hundred out of the bank, intending to head for Indio and the date harvest festival, but he just couldn't make it past the Circle B. He got smashed and had to go to bed to sleep it off. When he woke up he felt too sick to go, and when he felt good enough to go he got smashed again. In a week his money was about gone, but he had sense enough to pay another week's rent at the El Rey so that he'd have a place to stay. The pearldiving was four hours a day for a dollar an hour and one meal—just enough to keep him in food and drink until we came back with a convoy and he could go driving again.

Ed regretted that he hadn't made it to Indio for all the free beer and free ass, but he didn't give a damn about having wiped out his savings account. It had worried him all the time he had it, and got him mixed up with the wrong woman and got him thrown in jail and caused him to miss a trip and made him sick for two weeks. Money was nothing but trouble: having too much of it around gave you the jitters and threw your life out of kilter. Goodfuckingbye to that crap.

Ed couldn't stand prosperity, but that wasn't his fault. It was the crazy country that couldn't stand prosperity, and Ed was merely living in the accepted manner. It was feast or famine, boom or bust, a big bender followed by a big head. Working for the Old Man exaggerated the tendency. For ten or twelve days at a crack you were pinched for money—staying in fleabag hotels, eating cheap meals, not able to afford a movie or a paperback book, living as though you were on your uppers. And when you got to L.A. you just had to cut loose. It was like a roller coaster—a slow grind up and a wild, fast ride down.

It was those downhill runs that made life worth living.

Born to be Free

Most men go through life az rivers go tew the sea,
bi following the lay ov the ground.
Old Farmer's Allminax
Josh Billings

After 1954 the Old Man stayed home in California and ran the business by mail and phone. He trusted me to handle things in Detroit: getting the cars and trucks released, hiring one-way drivers, buying towbars and other equipment. The last batch of taxis was in 1955. When the taxis ran out we had only Divcos for a while, but beginning early in 1956 the Old Man got some Ford truck business, and we were able to make three-way combinations: driving a long-wheelbase Ford, carrying a Divco, and towing another; or the front end of a second Ford mounted on the rear of the driven vehicle with a third Ford or a Divco full-mounted on the second one. I had been agitating the Old Man for several years to rustle up some truck business, but he was set in his ways. He had never done anything but run hookups of cars and Divcos in convoys, and he was afraid that he might not be able to turn a profit on trucks.

His old habits were strong. He didn't want control of the expense money to fall into the hands of the nomads and truck-bums who had drifted into his employ, so he ran three-ways in convoys too—usually three or four of them together. All the drivers were steady—no more one-ways, even on Divcos. The Divcos we drove then were the six-cylinder variety, and we decided that a hookup of Divcos that would run better than fifty miles an hour was too much for an inexperienced driver to handle.

This change to a crew of all permanent drivers made the job considerably easier. Everyone knew the route and the regular stops and how the job operated, and I no longer had to lead one-ways around by the hand. I knew the idiosyncracies and driving abilities and drinking habits of the men who were with me. No more oddballs, no more independent types who couldn't learn how to drive in a convoy, no more wise guys who thought they knew it all and weren't shy about telling me.

The Old Man quickly found out that he could make more profit per unit with three-ways of trucks than he ever could with cars, and he upped the wages—$150 a trip for me and $125 for the other drivers.

In the course of the first six years while I drove for the Old Man I saw perhaps three hundred one-way drivers. They popped up in Detroit, usually broke and getting hungry and looking scared and sullen and hopeful and suspicious. The ones we took on were relieved and grateful; the ones we left sitting in Kay Daley's office looked as though their last best hope was down the drain, and they'd known all along it would turn out that way.

We had men just out of the service, runaway husbands, misfits who couldn't hold a steady job, and fugitives from the grind and wear of the car-plant production lines. They were headed for the Coast to start over again or to avoid the law or because they had heard that California was the greatest place on God's green earth or because it meant that they would be eating for another week, and after that—maybe something else would turn up.

We paid the one-ways eighty bucks for the trip, and put them up in the hotels at night. Their only expenses were their own eats and smokes and amusement—which didn't amount to much on three bucks a day draw. After the standard deductions, and if they had been on the draw all the way out, they would clear about forty-five dollars—which for most of them was forty-five more than their previous net worth.

Most of the one-way drivers were never heard from again. They disappeared into the mob, and were quickly forgotten. But occasionally in Detroit or L.A. someone would approach me and say that he was so-and-so and did I remember him from a trip in the spring of . . . ? I'd say Yeah, sure, how are ya? And he would linger a while and reminisce about the trip and what a great experience it had been, and those were the days. In a few minutes we'd be all talked out, and he would say Well, see ya around sometime, and he'd be gone.

In the summer of 1956 I received a letter from a veteran of 1951, but without seeing his face I couldn't remember him.

Dear Pete,

Only to say hello and wish you the best at this time. I trust this will substitute for a period, in which I did not see you again.

This Sunday I called the Old Man to seek a knowledge of your address. He did relate to me of this address. He has surely maintained an extremely high praise for you.

I realize that it would be impossible for you to recall myself during a trip - Detroit - Los Angeles during December 1951. During the period which followed this trip I had inquired about you when I had the occasion to talk to Kay Daley.

Well Pete, the most important person is yourself! If you have a spare moment, drop me a line and tell me what is new with yourself.

In closing, I send my best regards.

Sincerely yours,
Chas. S.
'51'

Few of the one-ways had coherent ideas about what they would do once they got to the Coast. When we arrived in L.A., three-fourths of them asked to make more trips. Some asked out of economic necessity, but most asked because they liked the job just as much as they needed the money, and they wanted more of that free and easy life. The job paid sub-standard wages, you stayed in cheap hotels, you froze in winter and roasted in summer, and the worst part was going back to Detroit in a car: three or four men together, everybody smoking, sometimes stopping over one night in Kansas and sometimes going right straight through—about fifty-two hours from Los Angeles to Detroit. On paper, it looked as if no one would ever take a job like that. In practice, there were a dozen applicants for every position. For the wanderers and ne'er-do-wells the job was made to order: the first deal they had ever run across that actually paid them for indulging their natural bent—flitting back and forth across the country, just knocking around.

Those who were attuned to, or had adapted to, the normal mode of life were often surprised at the attraction they felt for a life on the road. They thought of themselves as settled, conventional men, working toward the logical future of retirement on a pension and Social Security. They may have been derailed by some strange concatenation of events, but it was only temporary—just a matter of time until they were back on the track again. It was a revelation to find that they enjoyed living out of a suitcase and going down the road—enjoyed it more than anything they could recall, and couldn't bear to give it up.

George Sanderson came up to Detroit one day in the summer of 1952. He was an accomplished cellist, had a master's degree in musical composition, and taught music courses at a Toledo high school. He was thirty years old, twenty pounds overweight, wore thick glasses, had a lovely wife who was an artist, and desired to leave the depressing northern Ohio climate. He wanted to compose, to play with a symphony orchestra, to live in a metropolis that offered greater advantages than Toledo. He was going to visit Los Angeles and San Francisco to investigate job possibilities and to gain an impression of the social and cultural atmosphere of those two cities.

We had a flock of taxis then, with two crews working. George made a trip as a one-way, and liked it so well that he asked to make another trip. After all, he reasoned, it was the summer vacation and school was out, so if he made a trip at the then-prevailing wage of $115 he would have enough extra money to stay an additional week on the West Coast and be able to make a more thorough investigation. It certainly was the intelligent thing to do. After the second trip he didn't even make a pretense of investigating the possibilities of Los Angeles or San Francisco. He simply made another trip, and another, and yet another. After seven trips he finally managed to break away from the Old Man and transport his wife and belongings out to California. George didn't belong on the road—not by his background, not by interests, not by education. Except that he was a natural-born truck bum, and he hadn't known it.

Another natural was Julie Crouse, who was a natural-born cheap con man and used-car salesman. Julie couldn't make a move without trying to turn a profit—a couple of fast bucks here, a tainted dime there, anything at all. You would come up to Julie and stick out your paw to shake hands, and as soon as Julie was giving you a fervent handshake while looking you sincerely right straight in the eye, he would clutch your right elbow with his left hand and lead you over to the latest item of merchandise he was peddling—or around a corner, away from prying eyes, where he would fish the item out of his pocket, lower his voice, and give you his spiel.

His line was always the same, and he never seemed to understand that anyone who had heard it once was wise to him. He would always have a couple of wristwatches with seventeen paste jewels, eight-dollar diamond rings made out of cut bottle glass, 24-carat lead cufflinks, antique knickknacks that had been made yesterday. Julie never saw other people—he only saw customers. Instead of saying Hello or Good Morning, he started out with I just made the deal of a lifetime. As he constantly inflated the value and exaggerated the beauty of the junk he peddled, so did he inflate and exaggerate his own personality and talents. Julie's idea of a redhot conversation was praise and awe of Julie; the only name he burned to hear was his own.

Everybody tried to butter up the boss now and then, but Julie did it all his waking hours: offering assistance I didn't need, buying my coffee, giving me the magazines that he'd picked up in barbershops and hotel lobbies. In every town we hit, Julie would head for the Salvation Army or Goodwill store, and soon would show up in my room to give me, free gratis, the fivedollar namebrand shirt he had just bought for fifty cents because he knew it was my size and style and did I ever see such a bargain, with no strings attached?

Julie all the time thought he was making mucho points, but his stock was falling every day. Going east by car with Julie along was like being held prisoner by a broken record—he never quit talking, even when we yelled at him to shut up. The only way to handle his noise was to turn the radio up to a roar. Even worse, Julie was a fat slob who had never used his muscles for anything but lifting a fork to his mouth, and to demonstrate that he was tough and virile he used the foulest language he could think of. All of us used a certain amount of bad language, but Julie did it without end, and it wore us out to hear about the fucking highway patrol and cocksucking taxis and the Old Man was a shitass and the people Julie didn't like were bloodycuntlappers and the weather forecast was for shit piss and corruption. Mickey said that Julie should go see a doctor, because he had a terminal case of diarrhea of the vocal chords.

In order to make his own star shine more brightly, Julie created nasty rumors about everybody on the job—and passed them on to everybody else, portraying himself as the honorable, decent fellow who hated to be the bearer of bad news but felt that the truth must be known. He agitated the other drivers and created some dissension, but soon we compared notes—and after Julie's fourth trip I told him to get lost. He was a competent driver, but that's all he had going for him. When I told him he was finished he wasn't upset, except to say that it was the result of a whispering campaign against him and he wouldn't hold it against me because I had been misled. Julie realized that I was young and needed advice, so he gave me two maxims that would help me through life: If you don't tootle your own horn it won't ever get tootled; and, You gotta romance 'em.

The last we heard of Julie he had found a home working for a flybynight usedcar dealer who bought wornout clunkers for fifty or a hundred bucks, gave them a one-coat paint job, blackened the tires, polished the chrome, steam-cleaned the engines, put heavy oil in the crankcase, slapped on plastic seatcovers, and sold them for several hundred—which was a lot of romance.

There was Norm Jones, who was from St. Louis where he had worked as an apprentice carpenter. His wife had divorced him when their only kid was a year old, and he had been bumming around the country for a couple of years. In L.A. he had trouble finding work, and being hard up for money he had done a bit of shoplifting. They caught him at it, and since his only defense was that he was hungry the judge gave him six months of eating free on the county. After the six months he still had an appetite, and was thinking of moving up to liquor store holdups so as not to be a burden on public welfare, when he got to talking to some of the Old Man's drivers in the Circle B one night. They told him about the great job they worked on, but that there was no way to be hired unless you were in Detroit to make a trip out as a one-way. Norm started out the next morning and hitchhiked to Detroit. He got there in time to make the next trip out as a one-way, did a good job of it, and we took him on steady.

Norm had been mad at life ever since his divorce, and six months at the county farm had only made him worse. Even when he was laughing he looked angry, and when he was angry he didn't have any expression at all—his face would be blank, making you suspect that maybe there wasn't anything behind it. It always seemed that he was on the verge of violence, that some innocent event or word was going to push him past the limit and he would bring the world to an end. He carried a pair of leather gloves—never wore them—and when he was all wound up he slapped the gloves against his leg, steadily, for minutes at a time, as if he were trying to hypnotize himself or whip himself into a frenzy. But nothing ever happened. He always kept control, never had a fight. If it was an act it was a good one. The other guys on the job were friendly but wary, and strangers were downright worried and kept their distance because they thought he was a psycho.

On Norm's eighth trip we were stopped the second night out at Monroe City, Missouri, with a convoy of taxis. Norm had a letter there from his mother in St. Louis. Whatever was in the letter made him act even crazier than usual. He paced around his room in circles, slapping his leg with the gloves and muttering to himself. He kept it up half the night, and at three in the morning he awakened me and said that he wanted me to fire him. I said that I had no intention of firing him, and he demanded to be fired but refused to quit. He stood beside my bed for ten minutes, slapping his gloves against his leg, looking as though he was about to go off the deep end at any moment.

Finally it came out that in the letter his mother had told him that his ex-wife was sleeping with some guy, and there was talk that she would marry him. He's fucking my wife! said Norm, going slap-slap with the gloves. I reminded him that she was his ex-wife, but that didn't cut any ice with Norm. He was By God going to St. Louis and kill the sonofabitch, by which he meant his ex-wife who had no business whoring around, and maybe he'd kill his kid too because he couldn't bear the thought of *his* kid calling some other guy "Daddy," and he might not kill the guy because he could understand how it was and maybe he would just break the guy's arms or his legs or maybe one arm and one leg to teach him not to fuck around with other men's wives, and I said ex-wife—but he didn't hear me.

The reason Norm wanted me to fire him was that he thought I would then be obliged to pay him for as far as he had come on the trip, whereas if he quit I might refuse to give him any money. I said that it made no difference, and the thing for him to do was to quit in good standing so that he could come back on the job later if he had a mind to. He was much relieved, and almost cried with emotion when I paid him two-sevenths of a trip's pay, and wished him luck but advised him not to kill anybody—at least to get the story straight before he did anything rash. He said he had the straight story from his mother, and his duty was plain. And then, because he and I were on such good terms and he had just confided his true feelings and the most intimate details of his life, he showed me his pride and joy—a .32 pistol that he had been carrying ever since he came on the job, which was some surprise to me. He took his gear and headed up the street toward the junction of 24 and 36, where he would catch the bus to St. Louis, slap-slap-slap all the way.

When I gave the word to the other drivers at breakfast, Mickey said that it just goes to show that a boy's best friend is his mother. We avidly read the newspapers for a couple of weeks, thinking that any day we would read about a great crime of passion in St. Louis, but saw nary a word. We never saw Norm Jones again either.

Happy Families are All Alike

Marriage, n. a community consisting of a master,
a mistress, and two slaves, making in all, two.
The Devil's Dictionary
Ambrose Bierce

I parked Norm's hookup of taxis behind our gas stop at Monroe City, the Imperial station on east highway 36. The next day, near Newton, Kansas, I turned the keys and permits over to Ray Jordan, who dropped off in Monroe City from the eastbound crew and headed right back to L.A. and got there the day after my convoy. Ray was pleased to make a fast turnaround. He lived in Pasadena and had been married just a year and was anxious to get back to his wife who was a real hotbox in bed.

Ray was a sometime cab driver and an experienced heavy-duty truck and equipment operator. He had come on the job in an unusual way. He had been laid off from a construction job, and was driving a taxi part-time just to keep busy. One afternoon he was having a beer in the Taxi Inn, across the way from the Yellow Cab Company garage on West Third Street in L.A., when he saw one of our convoys arrive from Detroit. He was curious, walked across to find out what it was all about, was directed to the Old Man, and asked for a job.

The Old Man checked his references and hired him at once, scarcely able to believe his luck in getting a man whose former employers said he was honest, sober, reliable, and a good driver. Ray just felt like traveling for a spell while waiting for a good construction job to open up. He also wanted to get away from his wife as badly as he wanted to get back to her when he was away, because she was always trying to run his life and he hadn't been married long enough to get used to it.

Ray had married out of his class. His wife was the only child of a wealthy real estate man in Pasadena. Her father had money and she had personality, but she was short on looks. Ray described her as looking like she had been kicked in the face by a horse, although she really wasn't that bad. It was just that she was drab, and the parts of her face didn't fit together too well. In her social class everyone was supposed to be beautiful, so the odds were that she was going to be left on the shelf.

Ray had been hacking in Pasadena, and he had this ugly duckling as a fare. She was twenty-seven and wanted a husband in the worst way, and Ray, who was thirty-six, wanted a wife, because he found a bachelor's life too lonely. The real estate father objected strongly, and although he was still on good terms with his daughter he refused to have any contact with Ray after the initial meeting—which was okay with Ray who couldn't stand being around those stuffed shirts with their country clubs and their swellheaded ideas about what hotstuff they were.

After a year of marriage Ray said that he not only still liked his wife but had even come to love her a bit. Most of their problems had arisen from Ray being unwilling to change his habits, and his wife trying to socialize him by nagging—but they usually managed to compromise. What bugged Ray the most was that she protested vehemently when he farted in bed at night, and he said he wasn't about to hold it in because it hurt his guts. So they compromised, and thereafter Ray got out of bed and went into the closet to fart.

Ray was set apart from the rest of us by his habits and the circumstances of his life. He was married and had a home; he drank very little; he saved money; he planned for the future; he was on his way up rather than down. From the first, you could see that he wasn't going to stick with the Old Man. He liked the traveling aspect of the job, but his wife didn't like it and it didn't pay enough money.

It was tough on Ray to be thrown into the company of a bunch of men who drank a lot and were always on the make. Most of the other drivers didn't even have the same taste in reading material and music. Ray despised country music, but that's what he heard most often—those slopeheaded hogcallers, whining through their noses. His most profound dislike was for Lefty Frizzell singing "Always Late, With Your Kisses." When the other drivers learned that Ray hated that number they played it at every opportunity. It got so that Ray couldn't come into a café where "Always Late" was on the jukebox, because some wiseguy was sure to put in a quarter and play it six times. Ray started carrying a thermos jug in self defense. He had it filled at breakfast, and at the coffee stops he stayed in his truck and drank coffee alone, even on cold winter days. Anything was preferable to hearing Lefty, who must have recorded "Always Late" in a torture chamber because he was screaming and moaning like a man with his balls caught in a vise.

Although Ray would have quit the Old Man sooner or later, it was his wife who made it sooner. Having landed a husband, she wanted him home nights rather than gallivanting around the country with a bunch of drunken bums. She trusted Ray and didn't think that he would go astray, but still . . . we were the worst influence she had ever heard of, and there was no telling what might what happen.

She needn't have worried, though. Ray went to a movie while the rest of us hit the taverns, and he never so much as looked at another woman. But when his wife put it up to him that he had to get off the road or else, he got off. Home and marriage simply didn't go with driving for the Old Man.

Jockey Rides Again

> The best liar is he who makes the smallest amount of lying go the longest way.
>
> ***The Way of All Flesh***
>
> **Samuel Butler**

Mike Cordano made a trip as a one-way driver in 1954, but he didn't come through Kay Daley. He was from Chicago, and was in Detroit trying to get a job with one of the big driveaway outfits or as a city driver for a releasing yard. He wasn't having any luck, when someone wised him up to the convoys of taxis going to L.A.

By this time we had left Spink's, and we were having our mounting work and towbar hookups done at the K and B Mounting Service on Mound Road between Eight and Nine Mile, across the road from the Dodge truck plant. Just down the road was a steel mill that every now and then threw out huge clouds of orange smoke and a rain of cinders. Briggs had a big plant nearby on Eight Mile Road, and the Divco factory was a five-minute drive away. Everything had to do with building cars and trucks, and transporting them. If the car business ever went down, the area was a ready-made desert—complete with ashes and cinders, concrete-block buildings that looked like ziggurats left by a vanished race, the skeletons of long-dead vehicles, and an oasis, the Keeweenaw Bar, next to K and B.

Several of us were in the Keeweenaw one day having an afternoon beer break, when Mike waltzed in and said he'd like to give us the pleasure of his company on a trip to the Coast. He was in luck, because we needed another man and he could drive as well as the average joe. Mike was a little guy who was always talking and laughing; even when he talked too much he was in such good humor that nobody minded.

He had a Chicago White Sox baseball cap that he wore backward. Half the time he talked about baseball and Luke Appling and Shoeless Joe Jackson, and the other half he talked about horseracing and Willie Shoemaker and Eddie Arcaro and what a hotshot he was at playing the ponies and how he had a foolproof system for beating the system and winning a shitpot full of money. With all of that track talk and his turned-around cap, Mike gave the impression that he had just busted out of the starting gate. Somebody nicknamed him Jockey, and pretty quick nobody could remember his real name, or even that he had one.

Jockey's system was merely a rehash of all the other dumb systems anybody had ever thought of that didn't work. It required three guys, and had one guy with binoculars in a rented room overlooking the track and the second guy at the bookie's and the third guy at the track, and a radio and a couple of open phone lines—right out of a fourth-rate movie. The one time that Jockey had tried it, it had been a flop—but only because they needed more practice on their timing. And naturally they needed a bankroll to get started, because you had to be prepared to drop a big wad before you made a killing. Just like any other business, where it takes money to make money—which Jockey told us was the secret of success.

Ralph Tripp, a big beefy guy from Walla Walla, Washington, came on the job about the same time as Jockey. The two of them became friends, and knocked around together. Ralph had worked at driving, lumbering, and catch-as-catch-can all over Washington and Oregon, and had been touring around the country on an aimless vacation when he heard about the Old Man's convoys to the Coast. With nothing to lose and nowhere in particular to go, Ralph drove for the Old Man for almost a year. His car was an old Willys Overland that was on its third hundred thousand miles, and had such well-worn gears that he could speed-shift it without using the clutch.

When we were in Detroit, Ralph and Jockey tooled around town in the Willys, making half-hearted attempts at picking up some strays, but they were a weird-looking pair in an oddball car, and they never were able to score when they were together. They each had a line of bullshit that had been honed and refined for many years. Ralph's line was designed to hustle some woman—any woman—into bed as fast as he could without violating the local ordinances. Ralph would talk about being a big sawdust-and-knothole man from the Pacific Northwest, which was instantly believed by half the women he approached because they didn't know anything about it, and Ralph was never more sincere than when he was lying. But if the screwy-looking guy with the turned-around cap was along, Ralph couldn't make the connection.

Jockey's line seemed designed not so much to make conquests as for the sheer pleasure of handing out a sharp line. Girls working as waitresses in truckstop cafes were the toughest nuts to crack. All day long they heard nothing but blatant lies and sick lines from all the Romeos of the Road who were looking for a quick tumble in the hay, and they became aloof and contemptuous. They didn't smile at wisecracks, they didn't respond to questions, they resisted all blandishments and attempts at conversation. But Jockey had come up with a sure-fire line of patter that broke through the reserve of the most hardbitten waitress.

Jockey: A friend of yours said to tell you hello if I saw you here today.

Waitress: (doesn't respond to such a shallow approach)

Jockey: That Herman never misses a trick. He told me you'd be here.

Waitress: (suspicious but curious) Who told you?

Jockey: Herman. He said he saw you around town one day last week. That old Herman is somethin' else, isn't he?

Waitress: I don't know anybody named Herman.

Jockey: *Sure* you do. Everybody knows Herman.

Waitress: Are you sure? I can't think of anybody named Herman.

Jockey: He knows *you*. He told me all about you.

Waitress: What did he say.

Jockey: No secrets, or nothing like that. Herman's not that kind of guy. Said you were looking like a million.

Waitress: Who was it again?

Jockey: Herman. You know Herman. You see him all the time.

Waitress: I can't place him. What's he look like?

Jockey: He's a tall, heavyset fella . . . kinda thin . . . Doesn't weigh too much . . . has short legs . . . walks around on stilts all day . . . plays with the cats. When you see him you can't miss him. Said to tell you hello.

Waitress: Uh, I guess I remember him. What else did he say?

Jockey: He said you were A Number One. I know Herman from way back. Said I'd enjoy meeting you. My name's Jockey. I make my money on the ponies.

Waitress: (still suspicious, but more curious; uncertain smile) Hi, Jockey. Where did you say Herman saw me?

Jockey: Uptown one day last week. He was just cruisin' around.

I'll tell him you said hello. Well, it's been great meeting you. We gotta hit the road. See you next time through. Maybe we can take in a movie or somethin'.

Be seein' ya.

Waitress: (thawed out and confused) Uh, yeah—okay.

When we got outside Jockey would grin triumphantly and say It works every time, and Ralph would say You tell 'em, horseshit, you been around. Jockey would punch the air with his fist, and say When old Jockey hits 'em with the stick, they *stay* hit! Ralph told him that he wouldn't get into their pants by talking about Herman, but Jockey would be grinning away as if he'd just made out with the Queen of Sheba. He never tried to follow through, or even speak to the same waitress again. The next time in that café he'd try the Herman line on a different girl, and with the same results. If getting silent, stuck-up waitresses to talk had been the same as getting laid, Jockey would have been the champion cocksman of the Western Hemisphere, and other places.

Ralph warned Jockey that some day he'd pull that Herman line on a girl while her husband or boyfriend was close by, and they might take offense and cream his ass. Jockey said that it was so innocent and friendly that nobody would ever get mad, but Ralph said that sounded like famous last words. People in small towns had no use for fast-talking city slickers, and some morning Jockey would wake up and find his head out in a peapatch singing I Ain't Got No Body, while the band played Who'd A Thunk It.

The All-Bran Affair

What is food to one,
is to others bitter poison.
De Rerum Natura
Lucretius

Ralph's and Jockey's stock in trade was kidding around and mild practical jokes. They egged each other on, and once they had a running joke going they carried it along until it died of exhaustion or blew up on them.

When we were transporting taxis we stayed the third night out at Emporia, and the following day we would be in Hutchinson for mid-morning coffee at the spick-and-span L-shaped diner run by the motherly but no-nonsense woman. Jockey and Ralph got into the habit of having a bowl of cereal along with their coffee: Corn Flakes, Pep, Raisin Bran, Shredded Wheat, Rice Krispies—the whole line of individually packaged cereals. One day Ralph asked for All Bran—and that was the one she didn't have. The next time through, Ralph and Jockey both asked for All Bran, and she still didn't have it. She never had it, because there was no call for it. If she stocked it, it sat on the shelf and got stale. Both Ralph and Jockey liked variety and never ate the same cereal twice running, and ate All Bran only once or twice a month even when it was readily available. When they realized that the diner in Hutchinson never had All Bran they asked for it every time. The nice old gal was always sorry that she didn't have All Bran, and apologized all over the place and said that she would whip up some Instant Ralston or Cream of Wheat at no extra charge—but nothing would mollify Ralph and Jockey. They bitched and grumbled and ran the place into the ground. What! No All Bran? What kind of dump is this? You think they'd pay some goddam attention to the customers. I've eaten in some crumby joints, but this one beats 'em all. If we can't get better service here we'll take our credit somewhere else.

The nice old gal swallowed it all and never said a word.

We pulled into Hutchinson one spring day with the wind blowing about thirty miles an hour, and raining like a cow pissing on a flat rock.

After we gassed up the taxis we ran for the diner for coffee and doughnuts. Jockey and Ralph sat down and said they would have coffee and cereal, but they hadn't yet made up their minds about what kind of cereal. They put on a big act of studying the various kinds of cereal, debating loudly about which was best and arguing about which they had had the last time. The old gal poured the coffee and fixed them up with bowls, spoons, half-and-half, and sugar. Once they had the fixings, Ralph said he guessed he'd have All Bran, and Jockey said that sounded good to him, too—and of course there wasn't any All Bran.

Right away Ralph and Jockey went into their loud routine about what a dump that diner was, and how a man could starve to death in those parts because nobody had the brains to stock food a man could eat. The nice old gal didn't say boo, but she had a look on her face that could have knocked down a steer at twenty paces. Ralph and Jockey thought that they were being hilariously funny, and were breaking up over their own sharp remarks. As the clincher to this grand performance, Ralph reached inside his jacket and whipped out two individual packages of All Bran and said By God if this greasyspoon wouldn't give them any satisfaction they would just have to look out for their own interests.

They slurped their All Bran and talked loudly about how good it was and what a crying shame it was they had to bring their own and how that would be a good place for somebody to open up a decent diner. Jockey wondered out loud if they would be charged for a bowl of cereal, and Ralph said if they made a move like that he would call the law and see to it that they were closed down. Jockey said that maybe they should pay a little something for the bowls and sugar and half-and-half, and Ralph said that only a gyp-joint would try something like that. Jockey said you can't just pay nothing, and Ralph asked what was he afraid of, and Jockey said he wasn't afraid of anything but fair's fair—and Ralph said if you're not a-scared then quit talking like a man with a paper asshole.

That was the end of the line for the nice old gal. She had put up with the baloney about All Bran for the sake of not wanting to argue with the customers, and because she was a nice old gal, but she wouldn't hold for anybody using dirty language in her place. There was no passage between her side of the counter and ours, so she grabbed a meat cleaver and busted out the back door and came running around the side of the building. A couple of farmers and the rest of us drivers jumped up and crammed ourselves into a corner of the diner so as to get as far from

Ralph and Jockey as possible, and Ralph and Jockey busted out the front door just in time and tore down the street in the wind and rain with the nice old gal and her cleaver one jump behind them.

She had surprising speed for a short stretch, but after half a block she was winded and had to give up the chase. Ralph and Jockey sprinted for two blocks before they even glanced around, and by then they looked as if they had taken a bath with their clothes on. The nice old gal walked slowly back in the rain, took up her stand behind the counter, said that she was going to close up temporarily so that she could go home and put on a dry uniform, and announced that if anybody ever asked for All Bran in her place again she would brain them.

The other guys razzed Jockey and Ralph about the All Bran Affair all the way to the Coast. It got under Ralph's skin, and when we hit L.A. he said screw this fuckin' job, and he went back to the Pacific Northwest where he could do a man's work instead of beating his way across the country in taxis and puddle-jumpers for slave wages, and if the rest of us didn't quit the Old Man we were no better than niggers. The nice old gal thought that she had chased Ralph two blocks, but actually she ran him all the way back to Walla Walla.

Jockey laughed it off, and went back to the Herman line. We thought that a happy-go-lucky kid like Jockey would probably die in the saddle, but unknown to us he had a secret desire to be a settled family man. We had a lull for a couple of months, and Jockey stayed in L.A. and got a job driving city delivery for an air-freight outfit. When the Old Man's business got rolling again, Jockey wasn't interested in going on the road. He had met a nice Italian girl, and was going to get married.

She was nice all right, and a great cook, and had big tits and a hind end you could really get a grip on, and had three kids from a previous marriage and an iron will and was just the woman to provide Jockey with a home and family and make him buckle down and toe the line, so they got hitched. Several times when we were in town Jockey came down to the bar at the El Rey Hotel for a beer or two, but once he stayed until midnight and got plastered. His old lady said never again, and after that he turned his whole paycheck over to her, and had to quit seeing us or she would throw him out on his ear.

The Kid with the Jealous Eyes

> Man is the only animal that eats when he is not hungry, drinks when he is not thirsty, and makes love at all seasons.
>
> **Anonymous**

Those few of the Old Man's drivers who planned for the future usually were able to follow through and realize their ambitions. Vic Szafranski and Glenn Miles did, and so did Ray Jordan—with a strong shove from his wife. Some others, such as Jockey and Ernie Jeska, had wound up with homes and families and steady jobs, but it had been accidental—a matter of happening to be in the right place at the right time, and being struck by a bolt of good fortune rather than ill. For the great majority, though, life was happenstance—just one damned thing after another.

What you got was what came along. It wasn't anything you could control or predict, so why worry? When good things happened you were pleased or elated; when bad things happened you were glum or disgusted, but relieved it hadn't been worse; and if nothing much at all happened you were content to be eating regular and out of harm's way. And because bad luck was only bad luck, and not the result of someone trying to do you dirt, no one got angry or bitter when things went wrong—when you were broke or hungry or cold. That was life. You took the good with the bad, and it was never more or less than what you expected. Everything that happened fell within the normal range of expectations, which wasn't wide—just wide enough to stick out your arms and flail around to keep from going under. Some of the Old Man's drivers had lived most of their adult lives without knowing how they would be eating a month in the future—or sometimes only a week or a day, when there was no work and the future was closing in. If I had been in that fix I would have been in a constant state of panic, and my only thought would have been to work at anything at all and get some money in the bank, so as to create a sense of security and to put my mind at ease. I never understood how the hand-to-mouth crowd stood the strain, but they seemed to stand it in fine shape and took the attitude of Something Will Turn Up, and what the hell. There might be discomfort and boredom and craving for what you couldn't have, but no matter how bad it got you didn't figure to be entirely without food, clothing, and shelter. It was a great country, and there was bound to be a lucky break sometime.

The Kid With the Jealous Eyes got off the Holbrook bus one day at K and B Mounting, looking to make a trip to L.A. because he was down and out and was tired of eating the slop his old lady served up with what they got on welfare. Neither he nor his old lady had done a lick of work in six months, which was okay because they were getting by, but his old lady was pissed off because he was screwing a sixteen-year-old girl who lived in the next block, and she was all the time getting on him about it. The Kid was a nice guy and easygoing, but he threatened to slap her silly if she didn't get off his back. With things getting that bad, the Kid figured that he'd better bug out for a spell until she cooled off.

His name was Clyde Henney. He couldn't read or write, and had the worst crossed eyes we had ever seen. They seemed to be watching each other, which is how Freeman came to name him on the first day we saw him—and thereafter he was known as The Kid. With all his obvious drawbacks you'd think that he was worse handicapped than a three-legged horse with the blind staggers, and although he couldn't land a good job he sure had phenomenal success with girls. We took him on as a one-way driver, and right off he told us about his old lady and his girlfriend and the rest of his girlfriends that his old lady didn't know anything about but were so numerous that he had to hire an accountant to keep track of them.

Of course no one believed stories like that, so on the morning that we were leaving town with the convoy The Kid brought his sixteen-year-old around to give us an eyeful. She looked like Miss America, wore shorts and a blouse that were a couple of sizes too small, and didn't have the first sign of a brain. Her only expression was a vacuous smile, and she never talked except to say yes or no in answer to a question. The Kid always talked about his girlfriends as though they weren't present, and he encouraged us to offer her a couple of bucks for a quick fuck, saying that she was okay and kept herself clean but she had a cunt like a mare and was accustomed to take a douche with a garden hose. Under the circumstances, no one felt like making her an offer. The girl gave us the empty smile, which meant yes, no, and who cares.

On later trips, when The Kid was one of the steady drivers, he would show up at K and B with a different girl every time. There seemed to be an inexhaustible supply of the same type: young, dumb, stacked, and servile. While we spent the day getting our hookups ready to go—installing clearance lights, windshield covers, safety chains—The Kid's girl would sit dumbly, not doing or saying anything, smiling when spoken to. Invariably The Kid told us tales of his latest exploits or feats of derring-do. "I fucked Marylou on the livingroom couch while my old lady was in the kitchen cooking supper." "We got caught by a long freight train at the grade crossing on Mt. Elliott, and she jacked me off while we were waiting." "My old lady passed out from too many beers, and I screwed Betty in the same bed—and then I screwed my old lady and she didn't even wake up."

Coming from most guys, stories like that would have been loud-mouthed bragging or signs of a rich fantasy life, but coming from The Kid we felt that they were true. He wasn't boasting—just matter-of-factly recounting the day's activities. When you have a lot of time on your hands and no money for travel or entertainment, you have to fill up the time with something. What The Kid engaged in was the business of people who have no other business. We never saw The Kid's old lady, but from his description she weighed over two hundred pounds, had sauerkraut breath, and an awful gash—looked like she'd been hit in the crotch with a broadax.

The Kid made ten or twelve trips with Divcos and taxis, and then he too got fouled up in Las Vegas, New Mexico. He made out with a Mexican girl who worked as a waitress at the Red Ball Café on the main drag. Whatever The Kid's appeal was, it seemed to work on girls everywhere. Perhaps he had an instinct for girls who were desperate—who wanted a guy who would spend some money on them and hold out the hope of helping them to escape from their dull surroundings and boring lives. The Kid was free with money when he had it, and any girl in Las Vegas in her right mind wanted to escape, although most of them thought only about escaping to Santa Fe or Albuquerque.

The Kid convinced this girl that he wanted to marry her and take her back to Detroit, but he neglected to tell her that he was already married. He took her to Detroit and installed her in the same house with his old lady, and said he didn't want to take any sass from either of them or he would give them a fat lip. The Mexican girl didn't know anyone in Detroit, she didn't speak English very well, she hated the climate, couldn't eat the food, and was afraid to go out of the house by herself. The Kid quit driving for the Old Man and stayed home to take care of his old lady and his hot tamale and all his other girlfriends—which amounted to full-time work—but there was no money coming in so they had to go back on welfare.

The Mexican girl gradually became bolder, and even more desperate to escape Detroit than she had been Las Vegas. She didn't have enough money to buy herself a ticket to anywhere, so she began to agitate The Kid to take her back to New Mexico where she could be with her own kind of people and get some food she could eat. True to his word, The Kid gave her a fat lip a couple of times, but to show that he didn't bear a grudge he would fuck her immediately after he clobbered her, which encouraged her to keep on agitating. The Kid's old lady joined in the agitation, and after several months The Kid caved in and agreed to take the Mexican girl back home.

He went to a usedcar lot that dealt exclusively in wornout junkers where you could get a hunk of rusted iron for ten dollars down and five a week. They had a 1947 Studebaker for seventy-five bucks. The Kid paid his ten and left town with the Mexican girl, and the usedcar crumbs never saw him again. He started out the same day that I left town with a convoy of taxis, and we saw him and the girl on the road every day because the Studebaker had a worn frontend and rods that were about to let loose, and The Kid was afraid to drive it faster than forty-five. The car took a quart of oil every fifty or sixty miles. The Kid got drain oil from service stations, which were glad to give it to him for nothing and get it off their hands. He had enough money for gas and food but not enough for hotels, so he and the girl slept in the car—which was okay because it was summer and the only trouble was the flies and mosquitoes.

When they got to Las Vegas they were back in the clutches of true love again, and the girl remembered why she had wanted to escape that burg, so they decided to head on down to Albuquerque and make a go of it there. When I got to the end of the Santa Fe truck bypass with the convoy, there was The Kid, sitting on the fender of his Studebaker, with no gas and no money. He bummed a dime from each member of the convoy and got together enough money to buy a gallon and a half of gas and a gallon of diesel fuel, and smoked his way to Albuquerque by coasting down the hills.

The next morning he got a job washing cars for the Ford dealer. He and his tamale lived in his car for two weeks, but when The Kid got his first full pay they moved into a motel with kitchenette—and were on their way up. But it was too good to be true. Neither one could stand the food the other liked. The Kid wanted to fuck twice a day, but the girl thought that anything more than twice a week was indecent and maybe even against the church. She wanted The Kid to take a shower every other day, but The Kid said that two or three times a month was enough because hot water made him weak. It's those little things that will get you in the end.

One day when The Kid was at work, the girl packed her gear and took the bus back to Las Vegas, which was home if nothing else. The Kid knew when he was well off, so he got some more drain oil and headed for the Coast. He made it to Prescott, Arizona, ran out of money again, got a job doing pick and shovel work, and stayed a couple of weeks. Then he plugged along to Indio where he ran into Ernie Jeska, one of the Old Man's former drivers.

Ernie had found out early in life that he didn't have to make plans or choices or think about the consequences of his next move—it was all out of his hands. Ernie was from Ypsi, and his buddy Fat had steered him to the Old Man's operation. When business was slow and he was laid off, he went to Indio because he liked the hot weather. He bought a used panel truck for $150, and went to work running wetbacks from the border to Bakersfield, making three rounds a week. He was on good terms with the Border Patrol, but they told him that he would have to quit doing that or else the judge would put him so far back they would have to pipe sunlight to him, and they steered him to an honest job hauling hay. While on that job he met a divorced woman with five kids who owned a modest ranch in the Coachella Valley south of Indio. She was getting along okay except that she wanted a man around the house, and Ernie was doing all right except that he was sure tired of one-night stands.

They got married. Ernie kept on driving and she ran the ranch, and there it was eight years after the war and Ernie had a home and a wife and a readymade family and a good job. He was sure sitting pretty, but life had been just one damned thing after another, and he had no idea how he'd got there.

When The Kid hit town and ran into Ernie at a café, they went out to the Sealevel Palms bar and The Kid drank up all his money.

I was running my fourth convoy since The Kid and his tamale had left Detroit. On the last day of the trip we pulled into the Signal Hill truck stop a few miles west of Indio—and there was The Kid, hoping to bum enough nickels and dimes to buy gas to go to L.A. He said that his old Studebaker was holding up great, but that it had developed the strangest symptom in the frontend that he had ever seen, and without being asked he gave us a demonstration.

He gunned the engine and came across the dirt parking lot making about twenty miles an hour in first gear, and suddenly made a tight U-turn. The front wheels cocked over at an angle of sixty degrees, and the car didn't pull out of the turn—it just went around and around in a circle. The Kid propped the hand throttle open with a matchstick, and climbed into the back seat. The engine roared, the front tires squealed against the fenders, the driverless car wheeled around in a circle throwing sand and dust in the air, and The Kid sat in the middle of the back seat, his eyes staring at each other and a huge grin on his face, looking like a crazy monarch presiding over the end of the automobile age.

It was the Studebaker's last fling. A fan blade snapped off and gouged into the radiator, and the shock of the unbalanced fan was too much for the bearings. The engine gulped and coughed, threw a rod, froze up tight, and the car came to an abrupt halt, throwing The Kid into the front seat. Everybody hollered and cheered, and The Kid crawled out with his forehead bruised from hitting the dashpanel, but it had been a spectacular grand finale and he was still grinning like an ape.

The front wheels of the car were slued hard to the left and were almost horizontal, steam and rusty liquid were spurting from the ruined radiator, and a last wisp of oily smoke drifted from the tailpipe. The car was done for, and would have to be buried where it lay. The Kid said it was the best ten-dollar car he had ever owned, and he would shop around to see if he couldn't find another one like it. Being as The Kid was broke and stranded, I gave him a ride to L.A.—and he went back driving for the Old Man.

The Last of the Bourbons

"Do other men for what they would do you."
That's the true business precept.
Martin Chuzzlewit
Charles Dickens

We were all agreed that employers were the strangest bunch of people ever to come down the pike. With most of them you could see how they got to be the owner or the boss of some enterprise: it took single-mindedness, selfishness, and stubbornness. You kept your hand upon the dollar and your eye upon the balance sheet—and the devil take the hindmost. The hindmost were your employees, which we knew all about because we were there.

The Old Man, like most other employers, figured that because he understood his own business and was operating in the black, he was an expert in all other fields. From the hindmost point of view it was plain that the Old Man didn't know much about anything, and a lot of what he did know he didn't understand. He was so busy tending to business that he had no time to learn anything new, and if by accident he picked up some new information he always interpreted it in the light of what he knew from running his own business—which meant that he had a misconception about what happened in most other realms.

The Old Man and other employers were dead certain that they knew all there was to know about their employees—and they were all of them dead wrong. None of us had ever yet run onto a boss who knew the first thing about his hired help. Least of all did the Old Man understand why anyone wanted to work for him, at the wages he paid. He actually thought that he paid good wages, and didn't believe me when I told him what union scale was. I acquired a copy of Local 299's contract, and the Old Man still didn't want to believe it. He darkly implied that it wasn't possible to pay that much, and that there was something fishy about it—some kind of hoax that he couldn't quite figure out.

The Old Man regarded himself as a decent, fair-minded man, and thought that his employees looked on him in the same way. He thought that his employees regarded driving for him as a privilege—as well they should, he thought—but that's because he mistook their anxiety to make more trips as a sign that they liked his wages, and this mistaken notion was reinforced because there were always men clamoring to get on the job.

The Old Man had never been in the position of not knowing where his next meal was coming from, and he couldn't grasp what went on in the head of someone who was in that fix. Those men had to work at something, and driving for the Old Man was what they had stumbled upon. It was a free and easy job in a lot of ways, but it was underpaid and the conditions were lousy and the longer you did it the tougher it became—but you had to keep on because the day after you quit or were laid off you were flat on your back.

The Old Man couldn't see any of that. All he could see were the results: lots of men wanted to drive for him, some of them stayed for years, and therefore he was offering a good deal—and all the griping and lamenting about low wages and bad conditions were only par for the course. Workingmen weren't what they used to be, and had become chronic complainers, whiners, and agitators even though they were perfectly well off. If the unions had only left well enough alone there wouldn't be any problems.

The Old Man couldn't comprehend why everyone was eternally broke. About once a year he would ask me what in the world the men *did* with their money, and when I would describe how they blew it all in he'd shake his head sadly and wonder why they didn't learn from experience. I didn't have the heart to reply that they *had* learned—that blowing it all in was what they liked best, and if they were obliged to save their money and forego the joys of living for the moment it would rob them of the best part of their lives—and then why go on?

One year when the Old Man asked me what they did with their money I answered that they spent nine-tenths of it on liquor and women, and the other tenth was just wasted somewhere. The Old Man took me seriously, not understanding that I was making a joke, and he wondered if maybe it didn't make good sense to pay them *less* money, for if their money was only spent foolishly it wouldn't hurt them to have less of it. I countered by saying that it would make good sense to pay them *more* money, for the same reason—it wouldn't hurt them. That threw the Old Man for a loss, and we quit talking about it.

Some weeks later the Old Man came up with the idea of starting savings accounts for all the steady drivers, and each trip giving them only half their pay and putting the rest in savings. I replied that forced savings undoubtedly was illegal, and furthermore it was just as well that they blew their dough in L.A. and were broke when we started the next trip. Men with empty pockets were much easier to handle. The Old Man had run enough trips himself to see the truth in that, but he couldn't help fretting over the problem. He hated to think that the money he paid his drivers provided the margin of profit for the Circle B and other spas. He didn't understand why it should be that way. Especially he didn't understand that it was a problem only because he fretted about it.

Every year or so the Old Man would get it into his head that he could raise the caliber of his drivers by hiring them directly, rather than letting them come on the job in the accustomed way—making the initial trip as a one-way. He would put an ad in the Pasadena newspaper, and get fifty or sixty responses. The ad gave only a box number, so the applicants would have to write a letter—and the Old Man would at least be able to tell if they had their heads screwed on right. He'd interview a dozen of the most promising, and hire three or four—and the caliber was never any better than what he got by hit-or-miss. I suspect that the top-notch men got wind of what a pinchpenny, uncertain job it was, and backed away. The ones who still hungered after the job after they had learned the particulars were the same sort the Old Man already had—wanderers and bums and restless young men who wanted to see the country, and guys who didn't give a hang about getting ahead in the world and were content with an undemanding job at a modest wage.

One of the latter was Frank Greer, whom the Old Man hired in 1954. Frank was honest, trustworthy, experienced on heavy equipment, and a teetotaler—and lived frugally and saved money every trip. He was just the sort of employee the Old Man thought he wanted. Frank owned a bungalow in Encino, in the San Fernando Valley, which made him the only driver the Old Man ever had who owned his own home. Frank made five or six trips, and did a fine job except that he refused to take any initiative or responsibility—which puzzled the Old Man. Because why didn't an intelligent, sober man want to better himself?

What Frank most wanted to do was to read books and play the drums. He belonged to an amateur music group, and if he had any ambition at all it was to play professionally. But if playing the drums never went beyond the amateur level, that was okay with Frank. He had tried the route of ambition and hard work, and found that he didn't like it. He wanted to read, play the drums, and sit in the sun—that's what life was all about.

After those five or six trips, he quit—because he was ahead enough money so that he wouldn't have to work for a spell, and if he ran short he could do odd jobs. It knocked the Old Man for a loop to have someone quit when there was plenty of work and the man had no other job lined up. He had never heard of such a thing, and couldn't accept the explanation that Frank would rather laze around in Encino and bang on the drums. That was just plain nonsense—no one in his right mind would do that, and the Old Man wondered if maybe Frank wasn't a little funny in the head.

Three times in the next year and a half Frank came back on the job, made several trips, and quit again. After the last set of trips the Old Man said no more. Frank may have been honest, sober, and reliable, but the Old Man was spooked by such eccentric behavior. Someone who acted that way was more than just a bit peculiar, and the Old Man didn't want to be responsible for what he might do.

The Old Man couldn't figure Frank out, and became convinced that something dark and sinister was going on—which meant goodbye. Frank wasn't surprised at being given the gate because he didn't want to go onward and upward; he'd run into that attitude before. It confirmed him in the correctness of his own position. If the Old Man and all those others were so driven, and wished to drive everyone else, then they were the ones who were funny in the head. He, Frank Greer, had his priorities in order. If you asked, he told you how he lived and why, knowing that it made perfect sense. If you found his way of life unacceptable, he didn't care. If you thought he was right, he was pleased to encounter an enlightened soul. He never proselytized; there was no need. Life is nothing but living, and those who are happy aren't talking about it.

The Old Man thought of himself as a perceptive observer and astute judge of men, but actually he was a terrible judge of character. He rated everyone on the basis of appearance and money—and on one's attitudes toward money. If you had plenty of money and the right sort of possessions, the Old Man thought that you were a worthwhile person, and if you had a proper respect for money and weren't a spendthrift, you were cream of the crop. If you had money but were careless with it, you were lower in the Old Man's esteem but still entitled to a degree of regard appropriate to someone who had acquired wealth but lacked a decent attitude. But the prime criterion was money. One's worth as a person was synonymous with one's financial worth. In referring to someone of position or power, the Old Man invariably mentioned that he was worth so many thousands or millions of dollars, as though he were conveying vital information about that individual's character and humanity.

The Old Man described to me his encounter with a man whose Oldsmobile 98 we were going to drive to Detroit. The Old Man met with this fellow at a service station in Beverly Hills to pick up the car. When the Old Man identified himself, the other man simply handed over the keys to the car and the delivery address, and that's all there was to it. He didn't want to check the Old Man's references or to have a written agreement. He was quite unconcerned and unbusinesslike. And this was a man who was worth at least five hundred thousand dollars! In his own way, that man was just as baffling as Frank Greer.

Once you were aware of the Old Man's attitudes toward money, you understood his attitudes toward everyone and everything. The Old Man's drivers were chronically broke and scarcely had possessions beyond the contents of their suitcases. Consequently they weren't worth anything, and the Old Man treated them that way. He didn't abuse them or go out of his way to make their lives unpleasant, but even when he was being fair and decent he had in mind that the men were expendable, and if they failed to perform up to his expectations they could be discarded like bundles of old rags.

The Old Man had a different attitude toward me because he knew that I saved money, and because I was reliable and he needed me. In 1953 he started grooming me for what he imagined would be an eventual transfer of authority, with an eye to selling me the business and letting me pay for it over a period of years out of operating revenues. In addition to my regular wage and bonus for all undamaged vehicles, he paid me ten percent of his net profit. When business was good and we were running two crews at once, I was getting a decent income. But the more I learned about the Old Man's business, the more dubious I became about making it my own. After a year of being the Old Man's chief operative and junior partner, I told him that it wasn't the sort of thing I wanted to do for the rest of my life. The Old Man was mightily disappointed to learn that I had no more ambition than that; he thought I'd been cut from a better piece of cloth. It hurt his feelings, too. He had been cutting me in on—and offering to sell me—his life's blood, and I had scorned it. The Old Man knew no better than Freeman Morse and Ben Kuhel what the world was coming to, but that lack of knowledge sure didn't make him laugh like crazy. Life was a serious business, and no laughing matter.

The Old Man was penny-wise and pound-foolish. His instincts would not allow him to spend a dime to save a dollar, because he couldn't see past the dime. I knew him to go five miles out of his way to buy gasoline at two-tenths of a cent a gallon cheaper, and when you called him long distance you had to be prepared to finish the conversation in three minutes, else he would interrupt you in mid-sentence and say that was all *he* had to say, and to send him a postcard if there was anything else.

Despite much evidence to the contrary, the Old Man had a naive faith in the efficiency of the postal system—a faith that cost him money many times. He provided his convoy pilots with expense money by writing personal checks in the amount of fifty dollars. If you were running a convoy of eight hookups he would mail you perhaps two hundred and fifty dollars in Detroit to get you started, and provide further batches of checks at various mail stops down the road—at exactly which ones you weren't sure until you got there.

The Port of Entry at Leavenworth, Kansas was a customary mailing point, because we had to stop there anyway. If there were no checks at Leavenworth I could hope for some at Helen Voight's filling station in Hutchinson, and if there were none there—and I was running low—I could be certain of being resupplied at Buzz's Shamrock station at La Junta, Colorado. But if there was no money in La Junta, then I was stuck. Buzz would phone the post office to see if there was a letter for me there, or he would jump in his pickup and drive off to intercept the mailman on his route. If this didn't produce a letter I had to phone the Old Man, who invariably was peeved because he *had* sent the checks—in sufficient time to get there, he was sure, and he couldn't imagine what had gone wrong. He sent them first class rather than airmail in order to save three cents postage. He knew the collection times at his local mailbox, knew the train schedules, and reasoned that his letter would arrive in La Junta in good time, since it was on the main line of the Santa Fe. But the Old Man made no allowance for human imperfection. Often his letters were a day late, by which time I was in New Mexico. I would call the Old Man collect, and he would wire me some money so that I could get on down the road. It would cost four or five dollars and several lost hours, all because the Old Man wouldn't send the checks a day earlier or send them by air.

Mickey knew what was wrong: "The Old Man is so cheap he wouldn't pay a wooden nickel to see the Statue of Liberty do a swan dive into New York harbor and swim the Atlantic Ocean—overhanded."

Floating with the Tide

Now is the time for drinking, now the time
to beat the earth with unfettered foot.
Odes, book I
Horace

Most of the inadequacies of the job could be tolerated, or circumvented in one way or another; the only aspect of driving for the Old Man that we couldn't do anything about was the weather. It didn't take much snow to stop us, and when we hit one of the freezing rains that were common in central Illinois and northern Missouri we holed up in the next town and whiled away the hours shooting pool. In the spring the wind blew in our faces, holding us back and cutting down the gas mileage; or it blew from the side, threatening to shove us into the ditch.

Hot weather could be handled by suffering and sweating; zero days meant suffering without relief. Divcos were the coldest vehicles; they had drain holes in the floor and numerous other cracks and vents, and our feet rested directly on cold steel floorboards without even rubber mats for insulation. Our stops on winter days were dictated by how cold the pilot's feet were. When my feet hurt so badly that I could picture myself in the hospital having them amputated, it was time to make a long coffee stop. Neither the Divcos nor taxis had heaters, and thus no defrosters. In snow or freezing rain the windshield wipers couldn't keep the glass clean. We drove with a gloved hand on the wheel and a bare hand pressed against the windshield—enough to melt a patch three or four inches square.

The Divcos were solidly built, and seldom broke down. But they weren't made for cross-country travel, and their major fault—aside from lack of power—was a propensity for overheating and vapor-locking. Once the temperature was above ninety, a stiff upgrade would bring on severe attacks of vapor lock, and usually the only remedy was to stop and wait for the engine to cool, or pour water over the fuel pump and gas line.

One searing July day, when we were going from Holbrook, Arizona to Blythe, California with six hookups of Divcos, one of the vehicles began to vapor lock on level roads as well as upgrades. It took us two hours to make the thirty-five miles from Prescott to Yarnell, just before going down Yarnell Hill into the desert. The temperature at Yarnell was one hundred degrees. It would be ten to fifteen degrees hotter as soon as we went down the hill, and we feared that we might have to lay over in Yarnell and wait for the relative cool of evening. Mickey, who was back on the road after his latest stint of restaurant cooking, had a brainstorm. He went to the Yarnell market and bought a large, juicy grapefruit. He cut it in half, wrapped one half around the fuel pump and adjacent gas line, fastened it firmly with wire, and we took off down the hill.

The grapefruit worked like a charm. The evaporating juice cooled the pump and line, and we sailed along with nary a hitch. When we stopped at Salome for gas we checked the grapefruit. It was dry, scorched, and one-third its original size. We put on the second half and went to Blythe in good style. That Mickey was some cook.

The usual last day's run was from Prescott to Los Angeles. Winter or summer, that was the best day. In winter you knew that once you were in the desert the time of frozen feet was over with, and there was no more worry about snow and ice. In summer we were already in Blythe by sunup, and in another three hours we'd be out of the heat and down among the palms and the orange trees. There was the prospect of money in our pockets, plenty of cold beer, laughs and excitement, maybe some new girls at the Circle B—or maybe to change our luck we would plan to go over to Johnnie's on Seventh Street, or out to the Monticello to see what was cooking on the west side of town. Life was looking up—nothing but good times ahead.

The good times were as good as ever, but some of the drivers were wearing out and running down—and if they didn't cut back on the good times they were going to be sure-fire candidates for the boneyard. Mickey had always been a heavy boozer, with the ability to drink unlimited amounts and then recuperate with a few hours sleep. He still drank as much as ever, but his system didn't have the old bounce. After about his tenth shot with a beer chaser he would lose the power of speech. Normally Mickey was the only guy who could out-talk Freeman Morse, and when Freeman found Mickey in a bar, immobile and speechless, he would sit right down and call Mickey a pus-gutted Polack, a lousebound crabdancer, and all the other rotten names he could think of, because Mickey couldn't respond. Mickey would glare at Freeman and screw his face up in an effort to talk, but nothing would come out. He'd carefully hoist his shot glass, shove his lower lip way out until he looked like a drunken pelican, pour the whiskey in around his lower teeth, slowly retract his lip, and swallow hard. The jolt would pop tears out of his eyes, and he'd get a look of smug pleasure on his face as if he had just squelched Freeman with the perfect retort. After a night like that, Mickey wasn't able to function. He would lie in bed all day, staring at the ceiling, looking as though he had been clubbed between the eyes.

Mickey had spent several months cooking at Shay's Café on the highway at Tucumcari, New Mexico. He handled the breakfast shift, and Monday through Friday he prepared the entree for the Businessman's Special Lunch. On Thursdays he did stuffed green peppers, which had earned him a considerable local reputation. One of the businessmen who ate at Shay's regularly was so impressed by the stuffed peppers that he hired Mickey to handle the food end of a restaurant and bar he had just bought.

Mickey persuaded the businessman to hire Ben Kuhel to manage the bar, and it took the two of them just three weeks to ruin the man's business. Having many cases of booze under their direct control was more than Mickey and Ben could handle. They got drunk the first day on the job, and never quite sobered up enough to make a serious effort at running the place properly. Mickey couldn't cook worth a damn when he was hungover, and since they didn't keep books they didn't know how much money the business had or where it was. The customers were put off by mediocre food, the supplies of food and drink were consumed but not replaced, and with goodwill and inventory dwindling they could see that the end was at hand. At the close of their final night of business they cleaned out the till, divvied up the money, left the keys on the bar, and left town. Mickey went to Detroit to go back driving for the Old Man, and Ben said he would go to Phoenix where nobody knew him and there was plenty of loose money around and an experienced bullshitter could always make a strike.

When Ed Polacek was sober he strongly asserted that he would watch his drinking because he was no fucking bum and was not going to wind up on skid row. When he was drunk he said over and over again that he was no fucking bum but that his stomach had gone bad on him and he couldn't keep any food down and that's why the beer hit him so hard.

Ed had come on the job in 1951, and here it was 1957 and he was thirty-seven years old with his health not so good and he was worrying about becoming a bum. In 1951 he could drink a dozen beers a night and it never fazed him, but by 1957 his tolerance was gone.

We hit the El Rey Hotel at the end of a trip, and Ed had a beer before checking in. He bought a sixpack and took it to his room, and invited me up to hoist a couple with him. I tried to get him to eat, but he had no appetite. The first beer made him skittish and jumpy, and he paced around the room and talked a mile a minute about driving and the Old Man and the date harvest festival in Indio and would I please shove the chair in front of the window so that he wouldn't be in danger of falling out. The second beer took him from high to low, and he talked about his parents who had been hardworkers from Bohemia and he was from a respectable background and was no fucking bum and maybe he would quit driving and settle down and maybe get married although he would never find anyone as great as Rosie and if the kid had lived she would have been nineteen years old—and the one big mistake he had made in his life was to leave that ranch in Wyoming.

Midway through his third beer he lost his judgment, and there was no longer any chance that he would eat something. When I suggested, for the fourth time, that a sandwich would do him some good, he got a sly grin on his face and waved me off and said Don't Worry, Kid, I can take care of myself. To show that he was in full control he put his arms up over his head, rose onto his toes, and did a lazy languorous pirouette—and suddenly dropped onto the bed because he'd had a premonition that he was about to do a nosedive out the window. I left him then, because he was a lost cause.

Close to midnight he wandered into the Circle B. He had passed out in his room for a couple of hours, and was now drunk again and down at the mouth and asking strangers if they thought he looked like some kind of a fucking bum. He was getting maudlin about Detroit, which was the only home he'd ever had, and said he was worried about his brother and sisters and hoped they were taking care of theirselves, and thought he would give Rosie a call to see if she was getting along okay. We all told him to forget about Rosie and drink up, but calling Rosie and not winding up as a bum were the only things he could keep on his mind. We couldn't dissuade him. He got ten dollars worth of quarters from the bartender and phoned Rosie, even though it was three o'clock in the morning in Detroit. He did this about twice a year, and if Rosie was anything she was good-hearted because she always talked to Ed for as long as he was willing to put money in the phone. After half an hour Ed came back to the bar, feeling better about things and saying—as though she rather than he was the one with the ruined life—that he was relieved to hear that she was getting along okay and her three kids were doing fine, although he could never understand how come a sweet girl like Rosie had married a fucking cop.

It was the fucking army that did it, said Fat, who was in the same shape as Ed. When Fat was stewed he always thought about the army sending him to Germany where he had learned to drink that good German beer that had fucked up his life. He was eleven years younger than Ed, and it worried him to see Ed on the downgrade and on his way to becoming a bum. Fat could imagine himself traveling the same route.

Any number of times in the past year he had awakened in the morning unable to remember how he had got to bed. Once, just after the Circle B had closed at two in the morning, Red and I spotted Fat walking down Wall Street toward Fifth rather than heading for the hotel. He was walking with his head down, right in the middle of the street, intently following the center line. He paid no attention when we yelled at him, and we had to chase after him to bring him back before the cops spotted him and hauled him off to Lincoln Heights.

He wanted to fight us, but we grabbed him by the arms and marched him back to the El Rey. When we got him up to his room he tried to go out again. We threw him on the bed and held him down. He struggled for a few moments, and then lay still and in less than a minute he was sawing them off. We went to our own rooms, satisfied that we had done a good night's work.

At lunch Fat told us that he didn't remember any of that. What he did remember was that at five in the morning he had found himself at the intersection of Ninth and Flower, twelve blocks from the hotel, with no idea of how he had got there. When he came to, he was standing in the middle of Ninth Street, squarely on the center line. There wasn't another person or a car in sight, and Fat said it scared him shitless because it was like being in a science fiction movie where the city is empty and the people are dead and you're the last person on earth. By the time Fat had walked back to the hotel the sun was coming up and he was stone sober. He was so shook up that he didn't have a drink for two days.

No no, said Ed, it couldn't have been the fucking army. I was discharged in 1943. Fat said Your Ass is sucking wind. That just proves it. You've been fucked up ever since. It was the fucking army. *Everybody* got fucked up by the fucking army. The guys who were in the army are all fucked up, the guys who are still in the army are worse fucked up, and the guys who were 4F are ashamed because they didn't go the fuck into the fucking army where nobody who did go wanted to go, and you can't get worse fucked up than that.

Ed couldn't concentrate on what Fat was saying, and said he didn't feel so hot and maybe Fat was right. Your fucking A, said Fat.

Fat was feeling blue because the girl he had been screwing for the past six months was gone. He had met Judy in the Circle B. She was a lush, but she managed to hold down a job at a drugstore lunch counter—and maybe she turned a trick now and then because she had a bachelor apartment in an old building near Fourth and Figueroa and she was never entirely broke. She was simple and open and honest, and she had scrambled brains from too much booze, and just wanted some companionship and affection. She didn't care much about sex one way or the other, and if that's what Fat wanted most it was okay with her just so long as Fat would stick around afterward to talk and drink.

Fat propositioned her ten minutes after he met her, and she said sure, why not, and Fat called a cab and they went to her place. Judy undressed right away, and Fat thought he had blundered into a highspeed operation. But Judy had a screw loose about being healthy and staying in condition, and before she let Fat screw her she went through a series of calisthenics and insisted that Fat do them too or he wouldn't get what he was after. No work—no play. She said that they were the dynamic extrasizes developed by the Canadian Army, and would give him good muscle tone and improve his circulation, and probably make him a better lover if he did them with sincerity.

They both stripped, and for twenty minutes they did situps and kneebends and rotated their torsos and bent over to touch their toes, and for the finale stood on their heads against the wall for five minutes which was good for your brain cells. Fat said he felt like a jackass the first time he did Judy's extrasizes and was sure glad no one could see him, but later he got used to it and even enjoyed it when he realized that as soon as they were done he was going to get laid, and the thought of it was very stimulating. Afterward they lay on their backs on the floor which was good for your spine and Judy rambled on about the Canadian Army's philosophy of life and what a sweet old guy President Eisenhower was and how in order to be a good citizen you had to keep yourself healthful and extrasize your rights, and Fat said uh-huh, uh-huh, and they drank Ancient Age out of paper cups.

Several other guys had clothes hanging in Judy's closet, but she was open and honest about it and Fat didn't mind. Some of the clothes belonged to a swabjockey who was away on a six months' cruise in the Pacific, and there was a flyboy's uniform but he had been transferred to San Antonio and wasn't likely to come around again, and she couldn't remember who belonged to some of the clothes because she hadn't seen them for a long time, and Fat was welcome to anything that fit him. It was all the same to Fat, so long as he never ran into the other guys.

Fat didn't see Judy for a couple of trips, and assumed that one of the other guys was beating his time. But when we hit L.A. again and went up to the Circle B, the waitress there told Fat that Judy got hooked up with the wrong guy—a guy who gave her a big shot of dope. Her hands and feet swelled up and she went into a coma. They hauled her to a hospital, where she stayed unconscious for two days and then died. Fat got plastered, and felt so bad the next day that he almost quit driving for good. The traveling life was getting to him, and he thought that he wanted to be settled with a regular job and a wife and a home. But in time he came around, and made more trips. For a while, though, the spark had gone out of it, and with nothing ready and waiting for him in L.A. he didn't feel quite the old charge when we left Prescott for the last day's run.

A few of the guys had the ability to take life as it came without letting it get them down. Red lived it up as much as the Old Man's wages would allow, but he didn't abuse his system—just floated with the tide and took life easy.

Quincy, Illinois still had some life in it if you knew where to look—several of the taverns on Third Street had darkened backrooms partly concealed by beaded curtains. There would usually be a girl or two back there, a couple of tables, and the bedrooms were upstairs.

One evening I and my crew passed through Quincy on our way east. The other crew, with Red along, was staying overnight in Quincy on their way west with Divcos. We found Red in the backroom of a tavern, seated at a little round table. A balloon-breasted girl in her early twenties was sitting on his lap. The only thing she had on were panties so skimpy they almost weren't there—not enough material in them to make a pair of socks for a pissant. Red and the girl had already been upstairs, and would go up again whenever Red rose to the occasion. Red had a big black cigar in one hand and a glass of sourmash in the other, and between puffs on the cigar and sips from the glass he would lean forward and give one of the girl's nipples a flick with the tip of his tongue. Red looked like a big butter-and-egg man from Wisconsin who had cornered the market on all the good things in life. The tide was flowing his way, and everything was copasetic.

The Fruits of Labor

That life is worth living is the most necessary of assumptions, and, were it not assumed, the most impossible of conclusions.
The Life of Reason
George Santayana

We belong to suffering; when we misbehave it tightens its hold on us, we have its fingers always round our throats, which makes it difficult to talk; you have to be careful if you want to be able to eat . . . . The merest slip and you're strangled . . . . Life's not worth living.
Journey to the End of the Night
Louis-Ferdinand Celine

In winter we arose at four in the morning in Prescott, and drove off in the cold and dark. In summer we had been getting up a bit earlier each morning throughout the trip. We were up at one o'clock in Prescott, everyone bleary-eyed after four hours of restless sleep in the old frame hotel that radiated the heat of day all night long. The first fifteen miles were slow going—up and down the hills and around the curves—and then we were in the open and went flying down the grade and up the other side to Peeples Valley, and half a mile past Yarnell to Ross and Mary's Ranch House Café for ham and eggs or a stack of buckwheats.

From Yarnell the road twisted twelve hundred feet down the side of Antelope Peak into the desert, where even at night the air felt heavy and suffocating. At Congress Junction we angled right on the cutoff to Aguila, twenty-five miles of open going, not a building or a billboard, with creosote bushes lining the road and our headlights hitting the dark shapes of saguaros standing stiffly off in the desert. The main road from Aguila to Wenden was a straight shot of twenty-three miles, with dozens of trucks headed east toward Phoenix. Coming into Wenden the road made a sweeping S-turn across a dry wash. Just where the road bent to the right was an enormous billboard done in reflecting colors that could be seen from a mile off, looking as though it were planted in the middle of the highway: the Los Angeles Effect, even though L.A. was 290 miles away.

YOU TOO CAN BE A WEALTHY PEDESTRIAN
SELL YOUR CAR TO HONEST JOHN

On the other end of town was a smaller sign

VISIT JOHN'S OTHER LOT

It was five more miles to Salome—Where She Danced. A mile past Salome we stopped for gas at Monty's, named for its original owner, Jack Montgomery, who had sold out and retired to Phoenix. Monty's was now run by Earl Forlick, formerly of Columbus, Ohio. He had been an accountant for a big-time bookie, making a hundred grand a year and living in a fine house with four acres on the Scioto River. He had juggled the books in his own favor, and when they got wise to him he lost house and job and money—and he said he had to leave town for good or he would have lost his life.

Now he was grubbing along in the Arizona desert, selling cutrate gas, frying greasy hamburgers, and brewing thin coffee. The wolf was camped permanently at his door. He kited checks to cover his bills, hoping that by the time the checks had bounced around through several banks he would have the money to cover them, but he was going broke and was on the road to hell. He would open up at any hour for one of our convoys, happy to have someone to tell his troubles to while he made a few bucks pumping a hundred gallons of gas.

It was thirty-eight more miles to Quartzsite, with a metal statue of a naked woman in the cemetery, and the tomb of the camel driver Hi Jolly. A highway patrolman lived in a frame house on the south side of the highway. On the north side, close to the cemetery, was the sign of the man who controlled Quartzsite's only industry.

JUSTICE OF THE PEACE
Marriage Licenses

Weddings
Cabins

Twenty miles farther on we stopped briefly at the Arizona Checking Station at Ehrenberg to turn in our temporary registrations, and then we crossed the Colorado River into the land of milk and honey.

We went straight through Blythe and did the forty-nine miles to Desert Center, where we stopped for coffee. On the back of the checks at the café was the legend "Desert Steve offers free room and board any day the sun doesn't shine at Desert Center." We once asked Steve if he had ever had to pay off, and he said Yes, three times in thirty-four years—which was more than he'd bargained for.

From Desert Center there was nineteen miles of gradual upgrade to Shaver Summit, then fifteen miles of rolling country followed by a steep hill going down into the Coachella Valley to Indio. We gassed up for the last time, grabbed a quick coffee, and hit the road for L.A.—past the Signal Hill truck stop where The Kid's old Studebaker had performed its spectacular death dance, past Thousand Palms and up Whitewater Grade in the inevitable headwind, on up through Cabazon and Banning to San Gorgonio Pass at Beaumont where the countryside turned green at last, with just eighty miles to go. No more long grades, no more headwind, nothing but clear sailing down the hill into Redlands and through the orange groves and over Kellogg Hill at Pomona and into the smog.

We turned off the freeway at Peck Road in El Monte and went to a nearby machinery outfit, the owner of which was a friend and golf partner of the Old Man, and had the three-ways dismounted. In the summer, if we'd made an early start from Prescott, we'd be dismounted by three o'clock, and we'd deliver some of the single trucks to dealers in San Gabriel and Bellflower and Pasadena, with the Old Man following along in his Hudson to take us back to Peck Road.

By six o'clock the Old Man was ready to go home to dinner. I'd give him the record of how much each man had drawn against his pay, he wrote out the paychecks, and we sat in his car and paid off the drivers. The Old Man had a roll of bills in his coat pocket, and he cashed the checks on the spot. Then he told us when and where he wanted to meet us in the morning, and he went along home.

Each of us took a single truck and headed for town. We always stopped at a beer bar on Peck Road for a couple of cold ones, and then we chased the swarming taillights down the freeway to Los Angeles. It would be eight o'clock by the time we parked the trucks and checked into the El Rey. We had been up for twenty hours, driven almost four hundred miles, worked two hours dismounting the three-ways and putting axle shafts back into the towed trucks, and three hours more delivering trucks. Our clothes were greasy and our heads ached and we were just plain too tired to think about eating a decent meal or going out on the town. We gave the old bellhop four bits apiece to take our suitcases up to our rooms, and we went to the hotel bar to drink beer and eat a dinner of peanuts and pretzels.

The bar was full of furniture van drivers and produce haulers and haulaway drivers from Kenosha and Chicago and Kansas City. The jukebox was squalling away with tunes about lost love and wrecks on the highway and time done in cold grey prisons and I left my little geisha girl on the island of Japan. The shuffleboard and the pinball machine were getting a workout, there was a clatter of glasses and bottles, and everyone in the place was talking at once. Above the din you could sometimes catch fragments of monologue.

> ". . . over the Grapevine with fifty thousand on and I blew two inside duals and me with only one spare . . . ."
>
> ". . . had tits on her like the halves of a watermelon. When I saw those I just said to myself Mama, I ain't never comin' home no more."
>
> "Jesus, my ass is so sore I can't hardly walk, but before I let some sumbitch cut on me . . . ."
>
> ". . . pointy-headed bastard would write you a speedin' ticket if you was home asleep in bed."
>
> ". . . can't get rich selling your sweat to a . . . ."
>
> ". . . no worse than a bad cold, and penicillin is cheap."

We talked, as always, about the trip just past and the next trip and wondered what kind of car we'd get to go east in. Red said he was looking forward to tomorrow night, and Fat, who had been bitching and groaning the whole trip about everything under the sun, said he just looked forward to falling asleep so he could forget about all this crap, and this was no kind of life for a white man. Red wanted to know what other kind of life Fat had in mind. Fat said he didn't have the first idea, but working for wages was the worst thing in the world. And working for the Old Man's wages was even worse than that, what with never being able to get money ahead or meet some nice girl or get something other than the shitty end of the stick all the time.

Red said he was sick and tired of all the time bellyaching, and if Fat hated the job so much how come he kept on doing it?

Fat shrugged, and said if you don't work you don't get any money, and if you haven't got any money you can't buy any food, and if you can't buy any food you won't eat, and if you don't eat you won't shit—and if you don't shit, you'll die.

Looking Out for Number One

"there is some shit I will not eat"
i sing of Olaf glad and big
e. e. cummings

With luck, the flow of trucks would never end, and the Old Man would be too mean to die. With luck, we might eternally partake of life to the utmost yet not be called to account by either whiskey or women. With luck, life was arranged in a circle, and all the same damned things would come around ever and again. But when we backed off and thought about it, we could see farther down the road than that. Life was a straight line, and our luck was running out. The world rushed by, just one damned thing after another, right to the end.

The narrow, rough, two-lane roads built in the twenties and thirties were being straightened, widened, and resurfaced. They were starting to be replaced by divided four-lane roads that bypassed the towns, and we no longer stopped in Brookfield, Missouri for homemade pie, or gassed up at Max Ortega's trading post at Lupton, Arizona. The hotel we stayed at in Shelbina, Missouri burned down in 1957, our hotel in Emporia was torn down and replaced by a supermarket, and the old Green Lantern Motel in Blythe was bulldozed, and a glittering coffee shop sprang up in its place.

In 1949 the freeway came out of L.A. only five or six miles; in 1958 it was out forty-five miles, and there were just a couple of gaps to be closed to make it all the way to Indio—125 miles. The vast orange groves between Ontario and Pomona had been uprooted and replaced by tract houses. In nine years it seemed as though half the country had been razed and rebuilt, and if you thought what it had been like just after the war you already felt like an old man, like someone out of his time. Like the Old Man, or like the way Jack Blue must have felt in 1949 and 1950 when he was looking up the people he had known before the war.

The Old Man's business was steady: a constant supply of Ford trucks, with five to ten Divcos a month. There was enough business to keep two small crews busy, operating a week apart so that one was coming while the other was going. I had a crew of four, including myself, and there were three on the other crew with Red handling the money—for which the Old Man paid him an extra ten bucks a trip. The wages had been inching up year by year, and by then I was getting $175 and the other drivers were getting $140. It was enough to hold body and soul together, but still was only about two-thirds of union scale. In late 1957 the other guys again started harping on the three dollars for the union that the Old Man took out of our checks each trip, and since we had become bolder as we grew older I broached the subject to the Old Man. He said that he would think about it and let me know, but I persisted and the Old Man gave me his cold-eyed stare because he didn't like for his employees trying to tell him what to do. He said that he would have to check with his attorney to see how such a change might affect his income tax.

I reported that answer to the other drivers, who thought that it was a peculiar response and speculated that maybe the Old Man was claiming the payments to the union as a deduction even though the money came out of our wages. By the time we got to L.A. on the next trip we were adamant. Before the Old Man wrote out the paychecks I informed him that we were solidly against the trip fee, and that if he deducted it from our pay we were going to raise all holy hell. The Old Man didn't deduct it, nor did he ever deduct it after that. He and I never talked about it again. All of us were surprised that our victory had been so easy, and we were galled to think that we might have won it long before if only we had opened our mouths and put up a united front.

In February of 1958 we were in Detroit, getting ready to leave for the Coast with four three-ways. Ed had stayed with one of his sisters rather than at the hotel. He phoned me, said that he was feeling lousy and had a terrible cough and pains in his chest, and that he would have to miss a trip so he could rest up. The next time we were in Detroit I called him. He had been drinking too much and not eating well and felt even worse, and was in no shape to go back on the road. He was embarrassed at sponging off his sisters and his brother, and was going to move in for a spell with a niece and her husband. There was no work in Detroit, and he was afraid that if he didn't get some dough he would have to turn himself in to the Salvation Army because he couldn't keep on freeloading, and he couldn't take being on the road any more so I shouldn't count on him for any more trips, and that he was going to the hospital for a checkup. When we got to L.A. I had a card from Ed:

> How was the trip? Look out for all those rabbits at the Circle B. Tough here. You gotta live good and clean like I did and maybe you too will reach the grand old age of 38 and feel like hell.
> Ha ha!

In L.A. we heard through the grapevine that Ben Kuhel had been shot to death in a rooming house in Phoenix on Christmas Day of 1957. There was no way to check it out, but we never heard of Ben again.

The rumor of Ben's death strongly affected Freeman. It made him feel that he hadn't prepared for the future and hadn't been doing enough living, that he was in a rut driving for the Old Man, and that he'd better get off the dime and change his way of life before it was too late.

Freeman had a married older brother living in Macomb Township, a couple of miles from K and B Mounting. His brother was settled, stable, and had a good job. His brother's wife thought that all Freeman needed to get settled himself was to meet the right woman. A year earlier she had introduced Freeman to a recently divorced friend of hers, an attractive red-haired woman who worked as a medical secretary and was buying her own home. For reasons that I could never fathom, they hit it off, and every time Freeman was in town he stayed at her place. For Freeman it was home cooking and a steady lay, but the redhead was thinking about marriage and mentioned it often, which annoyed the hell out of Freeman—he had no intention of settling down.

On Easter Sunday of 1958 Freeman was at his brother's for dinner, as were the redhead and a dozen other relatives and friends. It was a jovial, festive occasion, with much rich food and strong drink. Freeman's sister-in-law teased Freeman and the redhead about when were they going to legalize their relationship with the sound of wedding bells. That got the redhead started, and she too teased Freeman—only she was serious and had the notion that in front of a crowd she might be able to extract a promise of marriage from Freeman. He tried to ignore her, but she kept at it. He told her to get the fuck off his back, but she kept right on in the belief that she held the best cards.

All Freeman's worries welled up at one time. Ben was dead, money was low, good times were scarce, life was short, and this goddamned redhead was trying to get a stranglehold on him. Right in front of his brother and his sister-in-law and all those other nice people Freeman hauled off and threw a roundhouse punch that broke the redhead's jaw and knocked her flying. Freeman stomped out in righteous wrath, convinced that he was justified because she had no right to run his life, and she had brought it on herself. By the time he got down to the Mt. Royal Hotel he had cooled off and was treating it like a big joke. He told us how shocked everybody was when the redhead went flying through the air, and how she wouldn't be cutting anybody up with her tongue for a while and would have to eat her dinner through a straw, and he laughed like crazy because it was a big load off his mind.

Right then and there Freeman decided to quit driving for the Old Man. He already had another job to go to anytime he wanted it, and he was in the right mood to make the leap. He said that it had been great while it lasted and to advise the Old Man to get out and spend his money while he could still move around, else someday he would die in harness and his old lady would spend it for him.

Freeman got a job with an outfit called Fleet Leasing Corporation. He would take two new cars or station wagons out of Detroit on a towbar, and deliver them to the salesmen of various companies—salesmen who were putting in upward of fifty thousand miles a year on the road, and were provided with new company cars every year or two. Freeman collected the used cars from the salesmen, and had the option of either selling them at once to a dealer or taking them back to Detroit, where they were sold at auction.

Fleet Leasing paid Freeman a mileage rate for delivering the new cars, and as an incentive to get the best price gave him fifteen percent of what he got for selling the used cars. If he couldn't sell one, at least he had something to drive back to Detroit. If he sold both cars, he went back to Detroit by air, train, or bus—whatever was fastest, even though the fare came out of his own pocket. The faster you traveled on that job the more money you made, and Freeman was on the road all the time to Pennsylvania, New Jersey, Ohio, Kentucky, Tennessee, West Virginia, and much of the Deep South. It was a job made to order for an independent, fast-moving, fast-talking, wheeler-dealer, and Freeman was in his glory.

One day in August, Freeman paid us a visit at the Mount Royal Hotel, to see how we were getting along and to brag about his lucrative job and his independence. Now that he was making better money he was living higher, staying at a downtown hotel, eating steak, and wearing sharp clothes. He had discovered an unexpected benefit to the job when he took cars to West Virginia and Kentucky, which was his favorite territory. Nobody in the small towns down there had any money, and when Freeman blew into town, his pockets lined with dough, he could get anything he wanted. The girls would fall all over themselves to get in the way of a spender. Freeman had only to walk into a tavern, survey the crop, pick out the one or sometimes two he wanted, buy them a beer, and then off to bed.

He had taken to carrying a cheap camera with a flash attachment, and always told whatever girl he had that he was a professional photographer and would get her picture in *Life* magazine if she would pose in the nude. At first the girl would scoff, but Freeman would grow more sincere, and intimate that it might be her chance to hit the big time—and the girls down there were so dumb and eager they would believe anything, especially if it came from a sophisticate like Freeman who was from the big city—Detroit via Chattanooga—and was generous with his money and drove a new car. Freeman was obviously successful, and you can't fight success—so he must be telling the truth.

Freeman had quite a collection of snapshots of naked girls in a variety of commonplace and grotesque poses: girls propped on pillows, legs spread and hands cupped under breasts; girls on hands and knees, hindends presented to the camera, looking coyly or sullenly over their shoulders; girls flat on their backs with legs extended toward the ceiling. The pictures of which Freeman was most proud featured a girl who was limber enough to be in the circus. She had twisted her legs back and hooked her ankles behind her neck. Freeman had taken several shots, including a closeup. He insisted that you could look right up her cunt and see all the way to her tonsils, and when we goggled in amazement he laughed like crazy.

There were also several shots of Freeman lying on a bed with a naked girl—taken by the second girl on one of the occasions when he had two. Freeman had some mild worry about being caught by the police with all those dirty pictures in his wallet, and had the idea that he would be treated harshly if it could be established that he himself posed for such pictures. Therefore he had kept his shorts on when being photographed —but his bare face was hanging out and the girl beside him was naked as a jaybird. I pointed out that there was no mistaking him, but Freeman said that he was okay in the eyes of the law so long as he had his equipment covered, and that the law was so finely drawn that they couldn't get you anyway if you weren't actually performing a lewd act. And if all else failed, Freeman figured that he could buy the bulls off with copies of his pictures. They were a frustrated bunch and would do anything for a cheap thrill.

Letters from Sally

It ain't your fault, and it ain't mine,
and it ain't his neither. We're all poor nuts,
and things happen, and we yust get mixed in
wrong, that's all.

Anna Christie
Eugene O'Neill

Ed didn't contact us when we were in Detroit, and his niece didn't have a phone, but I had a letter from him in L.A.

Dear Pete,
I have been feeling so lousy I couldn't get enough energy to write. I am working at Seders Bar cleaning up the joint after 2:30 A.M. and when that place is closed up it is very warm and while I'm doing anything I sweat like hell and then I cool off, thus I got one hell of a cold and feel sometimes like I did in L.A. when I had pneumonia and went to Sawtelle.

The next trip there was another letter from Ed waiting for me at the Port of Entry at Leavenworth.

Dear Pete,
I'm still not feeling up to par. This cold in my chest has really gotten me down, my weight is down to 135 now. Just feel punk in general. Alice and her husband got an apartment in Highland Park and talked me into quitting the bar to come and work over there and now they are giving it up which leaves me way out in left field. Kate has finally gotten married to a Italian guy who she has been going with for a couple of years, he owns an Italian restaurant and is strickly okay and we get along good. Him and Kate are moving into a small apt near his restaurant, and my brother Chuck is giving his apt up this week and is getting a room near the bar where he works, so things are closing down on me here.

The scene in Detroit was changing. West of Woodward Avenue the hillbillies were moving out and the blacks were moving in. The Mount Royal Hotel was sold to a big chain that installed a black woman as manager. The old Jewish people who had lived there for years were dying or moving out. Sammy the interior decorator passed away, as did Henry who ran the drugstore next door to the hotel. The new management made it possible for blacks to stay at the Mount Royal without fear of being given a hard time, and by the summer of 1958 the clientele, both permanent and transient, was half black and half white. Some of the Old Man's drivers were upset by this, but since nobody bothered anybody else they soon got used to it. In short order there were several black whores working the hotel, which upset the guys again. They weren't against free enterprise, but didn't think that black whores should be allowed into what they still thought of as a white hotel. Of course it didn't bother Red one bit. As usual, he floated with the tide, and was perfectly happy to try out some of that dark meat just to change his luck.

> Dear Pete,
> Kate and her husband have got a modern apt on Conant just off E. Outer Drive where I am visiting at this writing. Alice's husband is working steady and they have moved back to the east side of town. However I'm not working yet. It does embarrass me to keep writing you this, but since I'm a young 38 this can't keep up or can it?

Nineteen fifty-eight turned out to be a banner year. For the first time in the nine years that I had worked for the Old Man, everything went along smoothly. There was plenty of business to keep the two small crews working steady. And because all of us had been on the job for three years or longer it was like one big happy family. From January to March we were delayed several times by bad weather or breakdowns, but that was all the trouble we had. The Old Man went back to Detroit just once a year, to renew his contacts. The rest of the time he stayed home, and sometimes when we were all on the road the Old Man and his wife went to Carpinteria for a brief vacation.

Beginning in April, every trip went smooth as silk. We were always on schedule—seven-day trips one after another. Ford Motor had finally got the bugs out of the new truck plant that was opened in Louisville in 1957. Instead of breaking down in mysterious and aggravating ways, the trucks gave only minor troubles that we could diagnose and fix ourselves. We saw the other crew twice in every round trip, usually somewhere in Missouri or Kansas as the two crews were headed in opposite directions, and we stopped beside the road to smoke and exchange information about the job and accounts of our respective amorous and alcoholic adventures.

One evening in July 1958 in Los Angeles, while walking down Sixth Street, I thought I spotted a familiar figure going into the Greyhound depot, carrying a suitcase and a big toolbox. I followed him in, and saw that I was right. It was Max Jankel, whom I hadn't seen or heard of since the trip in 1951 when we were snowed in for two days in Beardstown, Illinois.

Max got in line for the bus going to Seattle. He was pissed to the gills, and when he got to the door the bus driver wouldn't let him on and told him to come back when he'd sobered up. Max argued and pleaded and threatened and cajoled. He *had* to go—it was absolutely essential—crucial—a matter of life and death. He had a job lined-up in Alaska, and he *had* to get to Seattle to catch a boat. The bus driver was adamant and said not by a damn sight would he let a lush like Max on his bus. Max began to blubber and moan. He didn't know why people treated him this way, his ticket was good and he would report the Greyhound Bus Company to the I.C.C., he would miss his job in Alaska and he had no place to stay and this was what happened every time a man tried to go to work on an honest job in order to better himself. A dispatcher came over and told Max to get lost or he would call the cops. I ducked out of sight, and watched Max tearfully enter the depot bar.

Hi Pete,
To tell the truth things seem to be getting worse instead of better for me here in Detroit.

I went to the Sally here. I am driving trucks in the garage and the warehouse so far. When I first went in I had to go to Herman Kiefer Hospital for a chest X Ray and a week later had to return for another one. I had a shadow on the first one and this time they took a bigger X Ray and also asked me how I was feeling and all my past medical history. I haven't been feeling up to par for some time now and my weight is still down at 135 and also I don't have the pep I used to

> have. I know after backing up trucks all day I'm just about exhausted and hit the sack early about 8 pm.
>
> Of course there is no drinking at that outfit but it really don't bother me. On Saturday I come over to Kates where I am now and starting next week I get off from Fri at 4:00 pm until Sunday nite when I have to be in at 11:00 pm.
>
> At present I'm only getting room and board and $3.00 a week but every week will get more money and when I get a route I can sort of make decent wages I guess, but that was the only thing I could do at this time as Chuck is not working and Alice and her husband are living over at my nieces on Eastlawn now and here at Kates is very small and also I don't want to make any trouble for her and her husband.
>
> Anyway Sally isn't really too bad when you come to really think it over. Of course there is strictly some real bums there. Guys that really don't want to do anything for theirselves and get a weeks rest and hit the bricks again.
> Ed

On a clear, crisp day in October, autumn coming on and the aspen trees a brilliant yellow, we were gassing up our trucks at the Hedges Oil Co. station in Flagstaff, when who should pull up in a late-model car, headed east, but Ray Jordan and his homely wife. Ray jumped out and shook hands all around, and said that we looked like a professional transportation outfit with trucks instead of taxis and Divcos. Ray's wife stayed in the car and smiled hello. She was uncertain how we might react to her, because she knew that we knew that she regarded us as a bunch of drunken bums who were a bad influence on Ray.

Ray said that the marriage had worked out just fine and everything was hunky-dory. He had been making good money and salting it away, and was now going to the brand-new town of Page where he had lined up a job operating a dragline on construction of the Glen Canyon Dam. He said that we looked great and I said the same of him, and said let's have a cup of coffee somewhere. He held a whispered consultation with his wife, and then said he couldn't do it. His wife had to take a leak something awful but didn't want to get out of the car and go to the can in front of all us drivers, so he had to take her up the road to a tourist-type coffee shop so she could go to a sanitized restroom. We shook hands all around again and said take it easy, and we went on down the road toward Williams and Ashfork.

Dear Pete,
Well I'm still at Sally's and Tues I will be starting my 8th week. I have hit the top grant for my job now $15.00 wk. I am driving. I have River Rouge, Ecorse, and Wyandotte for my route.

My next promotion will be going to salary, which is a problem in itself, because you have to show that you are going to behave (not any drinking) and can produce some weight on the salvage you bring in. If you can average 20,000 pds a week you get salary. My first week I got 18,700 pds and last week 21,900 pds. Salary will get me $40.00 a week to start plus bonus then. Bonus consists of 80¢ a thousand on all weight over 15,000 and 75¢ on all over 1500 pds of rags plus valuation on what furniture I bring in. Valuation is 3% on furniture. On grant I don't get these bonuses, but on the ten days I've been on this route my valuation has been over $350.00 which would have given me about $5.00 a week extra. Of course when and if I go on salary I've got to pay $20.00 a week board there (at Sally) plus income tax and social security. But I'll still make more than the top grant of $15.00

Herman Kiefer Hospital doctor told me the spots, I have two, were due to me having pneumonia those two times I had (1926 & 1954) how ever I've to go back the 1st of November for another check up. After I took a bath Fri nite I got on Katy's scales and went 129 with just my underwear and trousers.

Employment is not getting any better here at all, in fact it seems manufacturing is leaving here more so.

Kate and her husband talked to me about going out to the Coast with them and help them get started in something maybe an Italian restaurant, what they mean is can they depend on me to keep out of getting drunk and really help out. I think I can do it. I really want to any way.

Well Pete I will close for now and I hope to hear from you soon. I suggest you send your next letter back to my nieces on Eastlawn, as Kate and her husband have given up the apt and have gone out to the Coast for a look-see.
Ed

P.S. Some day I may have a more permanent address.

All Good Things . . .

> The Stars are setting and the Caravan Starts
> for the Dawn of Nothing—Oh, make haste!
> ***Rubaiyat of Omar Khayyam***
> **Edward Fitzgerald**

In late November the Old Man's business slowed down some. The Old Man laid off one man from each crew, and when Red and The Kid from the other crew got back to Detroit he had them wait for my crew, so that there would be five of us on the next trip out. It was the first time in a year and a half that all of us had been in the same place at once. It was like having a family reunion, and on the night that Fat and Mickey and I got back to Detroit we went out to the Clairwood Bar with Red and The Kid and had a rousing get-together. The talk turned, as always, to the road: the upcoming trip, how secure were our jobs, and how come, after all this time, the Old Man wasn't paying better money.

I knew what the Old Man's tariffs were, and we were familiar with the basic operating expenses. As near as we could figure, the Old Man was making as much profit from this low-volume operation as he reasonably could have expected with fifteen or twenty drivers on the road—and that profit was coming right out of our hides. It struck us that now we were all together we had the chance to hit the Old Man up for a raise, and could probably make it stick. The guys became so angry at the Old Man and his skinflint wages, and so enthusiastic about the prospects for a raise, that they were all for phoning him that very moment and laying down the law to him. But it was just the usual drunken palaver, and I shut it off by saying that we could discuss it again in the morning when everyone was clear-headed.

During the night the first major snowfall of winter blew into town, and in the morning at K and B Mounting there were five inches of fresh wet snow on the ground. The temperature was thirty, and a raw, damp wind was blowing from the northwest. Our three-ways were being mounted, and we faced a miserable day of slopping around in the snow and slush to hook up clearance lights and get the outfits ready to go.

In midmorning we retired to the Keeweenaw Bar for coffee and doughnuts, and to dry our boots and thaw our frozen fingers. To my surprise, the guys started in again on jacking up the Old Man for a better wage. It hadn't been just the beer talking—they were dead serious. We all felt that we deserved more money, and that there would never be a better chance than this one to get what we had coming.

The guys had about ten dollars apiece, and would be on the draw as soon as the trip got under way. I pointed out that there was nothing to prevent the Old Man from firing all of us, and hiring an entirely new crew. There were plenty of drivers on the Old Man's list who would jump at the chance to make some trips. But the guys were firm. If the Old Man fired them, then fuck it. They had been living before they went on the road for the Old Man, and they would still be living afterward. And they looked forward to the day when they could piss on his grave.

They decided to ask the Old Man to raise their wages from $140 to $175, and were willing to haggle over it and settle for something less. As for me, whatever I could get out of the Old Man was my business, it being understood that I would be getting more than they no matter what. Of course it fell to me to call the Old Man. I was strawboss and also had seniority.

We downed our coffees and the guys went back to work on the clearance lights while I phoned the Old Man from K and B's office. As usual, I called him collect, and of course he accepted the call, expecting to hear of some problem.

"We're all here together," I said, "and we've decided that the job is worth more money than you're paying."

"I don't want to discuss that," he said.

"Well," I said, "we feel pretty strongly about this, and . . ."

"I won't hear of it."

"But we . . ."

"Absolutely not."

I started in on my spiel, saying what union scale was and how we had sub-standard working conditions, and leading up to mentioning the figure of $175 per trip.

The Old Man interrupted me again.

"This is a strike," he said, and for the Old Man to use the word *strike* was the same as if a nun had said *fuck.*

"But we're not striking," I said. "We're just asking for a raise."

I could hear the Old Man's breathing, and knew that he was giving the telephone his gimlet-eyed stare.

"It's a strike," he said.

I started my spiel again, thinking that if I mentioned the figure of $175 we would at least have a bargaining point, but the Old Man wouldn't let me finish.

"I'm going to run my own business," he said, "and if I can't do that I might as well get out."

"But we're not . . ."

"You can't tell me how to run it."

"All we want is . . ."

"That's it then. I'm all through."

"That's fine by me," I said. "Goodbye."

"Goodbye."

We both hung up. Clarence and Elmer, the two Arkansawyers who owned K and B, wanted to know what the Old Man had said. I said that he had just gone out of business. Clarence said that you can't just quit business over the telephone in less than three minutes, and I said that the Old Man had just done it.

I went out to the yard. The guys gathered around to learn what the Old Man had said, and when I told them that he had quit business they couldn't believe it and hadn't thought that the old fart was crazy enough to do something like that. Just then Clarence hollered from the office that there was a long distance call for me. I hustled over there, thinking that the Old Man had cooled off and come to his senses, and although still angry would at least be willing to discuss it. It was the Old Man all right, wanting to know if I would do him a favor, and when I said yes he asked me to gather up his Indiana transport plates, his K.C.C. plates, and his Missouri driveaway permits and mail them out to him. I said that I would do it, and then there was a long silence with the Old Man breathing heavily and the seconds ticking away toward three minutes.

Finally the Old Man said, "Is there anything else?"

"No," I said. "Nothing that I can think of."

"Well," he said, "I'm sorry it ended this way."

"So am I," I said.

We both hung up again.

Elmer wanted to know if the Old Man had took his head out of his ass yet, and I said no, the business was all washed up. Clarence wanted to know what in the fucking name of holy baldheaded Jesus H. Christ they were supposed to do with the Old Man's fifteen Ford trucks, and I said that for my money they could sit there and rust. Elmer said that Ford Motor would probably turn them over to Dallas and Mavis, whose yard was just up the street. Clarence said that it didn't make him no never mind, because after ten days they would be getting storage charges of three dollars per day per vehicle and could probably make more money running their yard as a parking lot than any other way, but that half the people in the world acted like they didn't have any brains and the other half acted like they'd had their brains kicked out, and that he and Elmer should ought to sell the business and go back to Arkansas and go fishing.

I went back out in the yard and told the guys that it was final. We stowed the clearance lights and windshield covers and safety chains in one of the Old Man's footlockers, and I gathered up the plates and permits. And that was the end of it—we were able to wind up the job as fast as the Old Man. There being nothing else left to do we went to the Keeweenaw and ordered up the beer. It was noon, and the usual rush of men from the Dodge truck plant was in the Keeweenaw—men standing three and four deep at the bar, yelling for doubles of Kessler's with beer chasers. With several of those under their belts they were ready to face the rest of the shift. We felt contemptuous of them, because they were still prisoners whereas we had just been set free. We were grinning like chimpanzees, feeling ecstatic—drunk on one beer—and exclaiming about that being the funniest way to quit business we'd ever heard of and wondering what had got into that crazy old fart to make him do that.

The more beers we drank the soberer we got, and soon the reality came home to us. I was in good shape, but the others were almost broke, winter coming on, no place to stay, and no work available in Detroit. I decided to go home to Ohio for a spell to think things over and figure out what to do next. The other guys were all from Michigan but were unanimously in favor of spending the winter in California, and decided to get hold of a drive-out car. They pooled their money, and it came to just over fifty bucks. That wasn't nearly enough. They needed three times that much for the deposit and the gas going out and their grub and a little left over when they got there so they wouldn't starve before they found work. You had to have money to get a car, so I said that I would let them use seventy bucks of my money to flash around to prove that they were able to finance the trip. Once they had the car they could return my money, then scratch around to see if they could raise what they needed.

We had plenty of connections in the single-car driveaway business. Kay Daley didn't have anything, but Ray Orliman at All-States Driveaway had a new Ford Fairlane going to Hollywood so Red tore right over there and got it—and they were all set to go except for scaring up some money. Things were looking up. We bought another round, and everybody got on the phone to try to raise cash.

Fat got hold of his sister in Willow Run Village, and she agreed to lend him $25—they could stop by Ypsi where she worked and pick it up on their way out of town in the morning. Mickey's daughter was married, she and her husband both made good money, and they were concerned about poor old Mickey the lush—and there was $50 without even trying. With a lot of persuasion that was almost begging Red coaxed a $15 loan out of a friend. The Kid wasn't really expected to contribute because he had been broke from the day he was born, but he surprised everybody by announcing that he had got hold of one of his teenage girlfriends and ordered her to bring $20 to the Mount Royal that night, and she had By God better do it or he would kick her asshole up between her shoulder blades and she would have to take off her shirt to shit.

Suddenly they were in clover—money coming out of their ears—and were elated again because they were over the hump and it was all downhill. We went to the Mount Royal in the new Ford, bought a case of beer, and settled down in The Kid's room for steady drinking. An hour after we got there The Kid's girlfriend showed up with the $20—which we could hardly believe, never having suspected that The Kid commanded such resources.

This girlfriend was dumb like all the others, but she didn't smile when you talked to her and she hadn't learned to be properly servile. She sat in a corner and kept her yap shut, but when The Kid ordered her to open him another beer she said, "Whyn't you just bite my ass!" The Kid jumped up, grabbed her by the arms, spun her around, threw her face down on the bed, flipped up her skirt, yanked down her panties, and sank his choppers into her right buttock. She let out one scream that probably shattered windows a block away. We were stunned and fascinated, and couldn't do anything but stare at the teeth marks on her ass. The Kid calmly opened his own beer. The girl didn't make a move for a full two minutes, until The Kid told her to haul up her pants and get back in the corner and keep shut.

Mickey went to the market and came back with a sack of groceries: rye bread, Swiss cheese, kielbasa, horseradish, and kosher pickles, and we had our supper in The Kid's room. When the chow and the beer were gone, The Kid told his girlfriend to haul her ass out of there, and then we went up the street to the Clairwood Bar and got the party into high gear.

There was all the beer we wanted, and everybody was feeling mellow. No more strain and pain, no more freezing to death in unheated trucks, no more working for starvation wages. No one knew what was coming up next, but in the morning they would be headed for L.A. where it was warm and sunny—and that was enough. Something was bound to turn up. They were no worse off than on the day they had first come to work for the Old Man, four or six or eight years ago, leaving Detroit as one-way drivers on a convoy of Divcos or taxis.

Red said that he might try to get on with Yellow Cab in L.A., because the service manager there had always said that anybody who could towbar taxis across the country could go hacking for Yellow. The Kid said that he knew how to live close to the vest and would always get along. Mickey knew for a certainty that he could get a job—if his varicose veins didn't bother him—because cooks were always in demand. Fat said that he was thinking about going back into the army. It wasn't such a bad life if you knew the ropes. He would have twenty years in by the time he was forty-six, and could retire on half pay and maybe lease a service station or something. The army constricts your freedom a lot, but you don't have to worry about your bed and board, and the Eagle shits twice a month.

We were still going strong at midnight. Most of the other customers had left. There were two black whores at the bar who were giving us the eye because we looked free with our money and were probably drunk enough to be separated from it. They came over to our table and quoted us a price of twenty dollars. Red and Fat haggled with them, and they said they thought truck drivers were the best there was and they came down to fifteen dollars which they said was rock bottom. But there were no other prospects in the Clairwood, out on the avenue it was windy and cold, and finally one of the girls said that she would take on both Red and Fat for a total of twenty dollars. Red and Fat thought it over and decided that they weren't interested after all. The whore said Shee-it, we couldn't be truck drivers, because down in Louisiana where she came from the truck drivers had hardons all the time.

Fat reminisced about Judy and her extrasizes, and said that we might think it kind of peculiar but the strangest feeling and biggest charge he'd ever had in his life was standing on his head against the wall, bareass naked, with an upside down hardon. When the whores heard that one they got away from us quick for fear we were perverts of some sort. We didn't think it peculiar, though—we didn't think anything was peculiar that night.

Fat talked sadly about his schatzi and the good life they'd had in Germany, and he was sure sorry he'd had to knock her ass down the stairs. The Kid did some reminiscing too, although his stories were about what had happened during the past month. But they were good stories, and we couldn't fault The Kid for having such an eventful life that he couldn't remember any farther back than a month ago.

Mickey told the story about Floyd Aarons in Alaska, and the klootch who was queer for stale cake. Red could remember way back when, and he told about being snowed-in at Beardstown when Ernie Jeska tore off a hot piece in a cold taxi. I told tales of the old-timers—Jack Blue and Rummy and Buschbacher—and what I knew of the Old Man's operations before the war; and stories from the first couple of years I was on the road about riding the train to Chicago with Vic screwing this woman on the platform between the cars and Jim heaving his guts all over the hostess.

All good things come to an end, and we closed up the Clairwood at two o'clock and trudged back to the Mount Royal and hit the sack. We didn't make it out of bed until nine, and went down to the Mayfair Café for a breakfast of whatever we could keep on our stomachs. Tomato juice and coffee was all that Red and Mickey and I could handle, but The Kid was feeling so good about hitting the road for L.A. that he had peach pie and a bottle of beer—and it almost made us sick to watch him.

Fat straggled in five minutes late, and when the waitress came to take his order he said he would have coffee and American toast. She was puzzled and asked if he meant French toast, and Fat said no, just give me American toast and I'll french it myself. The waitress got sore, but it was just the remark to make everybody feel good again and ready to go out and whip the world.

They stowed their suitcases in the trunk of the Ford and got into the car and started the engine. I stood on the sidewalk and scuffled my feet, and we felt awkward and embarrassed because we didn't know how to say goodbye. I said that it sure didn't end the way I had figured it would, and that I would probably be seeing them someday. And I mentioned that it must be a real blow to the Old Man, too. He had been in the driveaway business for more than a quarter of a century, and now suddenly it was all over with and he didn't have anything to do with the rest of his life.

Mickey stuck his head out a window, gave me a sidelong look, and said, "The Old Man? I wouldn't piss up his ass if his guts were on fire!"

We all laughed like crazy, and then they headed out for the Coast.